Squirrel Tales to Game Trails And Shore Lunches

A Sharing of My Hunting and Fishing Experiences

BEN HARPE

Copyright © 2016 Ben Harpe

All rights reserved. No part(s) of this book may be reproduced, distributed or transmitted in any form, or by any means, or stored in a database or retrieval systems without prior expressed written permission of the author of this book.

ISBN: 978-1-5356-0103-0

ISBN: 978-1-5356-0407-9 (paperback)

Introduction

Though born in Michigan and having lived in many places, Ben calls Texas home. He and his wife lived there twenty-eight years and raised their family there. They have two grown children, both native Texans and proud of it. Ben retired in 2008 after more than forty-two years in the aviation industry. One of the primary reasons for his decision was making time for his family and his second love, hunting and fishing.

This is Ben's first attempt sharing his personal feelings and experiences on this subject, and hopefully it won't be his last. His writing contains a genuine "down home" honesty, a generous helping of humor, and is seasoned with just the right amount of emotion and sentiment. Young and old hunters and fishermen, as well as people who just enjoy the great outdoors, will find themselves, or someone they know, in the pages that follow. Ben not only writes from personal experience, but also from the heart, and by doing so is able to share his unique love and respect for all life.

As a taxidermist, Ben also shares a couple of recipes and excellent tips for handling your hunting and fishing trophies in case you plan to have them mounted.

Preface

Why do I hunt and fish? Because I derive enjoyment, satisfaction, relaxation, and pleasure from it, that's why. I enjoy the planning, preparation, anticipation, excitement, camaraderie, and if I'm fortunate enough to be successful, the meals of wild fare. I enjoy the sharing, the stories, and the memories.

In writing this book, I do not intend to make any bold or profound revelations for or against the sports of hunting and fishing. I only want to share a few of my memorable experiences in hopes that my fellow hunters and fishermen will be able to relax over these anecdotes. Perhaps they'll see themselves, or fellow hunters, in these stories and realize some personal enjoyment as a result. Some of the stories are serious, and some are silly and I hope will bring a chuckle. All are true, because I was there. The names have been changed to protect the innocent (me).

So please sit back, relax, and enjoy. And if you see yourself in any of these stories, don't tell anyone it was you. I promise I won't tell them it was you, either.

Acknowledgements

My sincere thanks to my father and mother, God rest their souls, my wife Georgiann, our daughter and hunting partner Kyle Marie, our son B.J., and all my hunting and fishing associates who made these memories possible.

Contents

Introduction iii
Preface iv
Acknowledgements v
1. My First Gun 1
2. Squirrels, Rabbits, and Ducks 5
3. My First Shotgun 15
4. Bird Hunting and Turkeys (With a Shotgun) 21
5. My First Deer Rifle 33
6. My First Deer Hunt (and Almost My Last) 37
7. My Second Deer Hunt 55
8. The Drought Years 59
9. Texas Deer Hunting 61
10. My First Elk Hunt 67
11. My First Caribou Hunt 77
12. My First Moose Hunt 99
13. My First Mule Deer Hunt 107
14. More Elk Hunts 111
15. Respect For Our Game Animals, Alive and Dead .. 119
16. Always Learning Something 127

Contents

17. Hunting Styles and Tactics 143
18. Fishing 155
19. Comfort 163
20. Safety, Rules, Common Sense, and Limitations 169
21. Slobs, Clowns, and Products 173
22. Taxidermy Tips and Good Eating 185
23. In Closing: Concerns 195
24. One More Thing to Think About 199

Squirrel Tales to Game Trails And Shore Lunches

1   My First Gun

   My dad didn't hunt or fish, but he did work two full-time jobs in order to provide for ten kids and Mom. His primary job was in a factory, and on the side he repaired cars and trucks, and ran a junkyard in our back yard. Being the oldest of the kids at thirteen, I was recruited by him to help in the garage. As such, I "grew up" with my dad and we became very close. I miss him.

   While in high school I hung around with a couple of other guys who liked to be outdoors hunting and fishing whenever they could. Since we lived in Michigan at the time, and hunting and fishing were still respected sports, I became interested and these guys introduced me to them. Since they learned to be conscientious sportsmen from their fathers, I got started on the right foot.

   Since my dad didn't own any guns, and since we were quite financially challenged with such a large family, I didn't get to do any hunting. Then one day a man agreed to pay my dad twelve dollars for a used part off one of the junk cars. However, he too was financially challenged and could only come up with six dollars cash. When he offered to throw in a well-used and well-worn little rifle in exchange for the part he needed, my dad took it. This surprised me.

What surprised me even more was when he handed the little rifle to me and said I could have it. He also told me that before I could shoot it, I would have to take a hunter safety course so that I wouldn't hurt myself or anyone else with it. Needless to say, I was one happy thirteen year old. That was many years ago.

That little rifle was in very bad shape. Under the dirt, rust, and scratches was an old Iver Johnson single shot .22. Both sights were missing and the rifle had been left in the trunk of a car for who knows how long, but it was beautiful to me. It was mine. Now all I needed to do was clean it up, take a hunter safety course, buy or make sights for it, buy ammo, buy a license, and start hunting. Only one problem: I was worse than financially challenged. I was broke. But I was also bound and determined to fix up that little .22 and hunt with it. You know what I mean?

I didn't waste any time getting that .22 cleaned up good. I took it apart, and carefully cleaned and oiled all the metal parts. I don't believe the bore had ever been brushed out, let alone seen a cleaning rag, and the outside of the barrel was rusty. With a lot of effort and a twenty-five cent bore brush and cleaning rod, I was able to stop the further deterioration of a fine rifle.

I also carefully sanded and stained the wooden stock so that it looked as nice as possible. I was able to remove all but a few of the worst "scars", and those that remained gave the stock character. It looked great, all things considered.

All the time that I was working on the barrel and the stock I was trying to figure out a solution to the problem of not

My First Gun 3

having any sights. I knew that the rifle was almost worthless without sights, but I also knew that I didn't have any money to buy them. After careful analysis, I concluded that the only practical solution was to make my own. I mean, why not? What could be so difficult about that? As near as I could tell, I didn't have any other options if I wanted to hunt with the rifle. So I made my own sights.

Remembering that I could not shoot my rifle until I had completed a hunter safety course, I now was faced with coming up with the money for that. No problem. My birthday was in February. I'd just ask for money, no gifts, and hope that I would get enough to cover the cost of the course. My plan worked, and I completed the hunter safety course in March. Nothing to it, right? Wrong.

I still didn't have any money for ammo, and I was dying to shoot my .22. Between my newspaper route, picking cherries and blueberries, returning bottles, and buying school cloths, I was able to buy a box of .22 shorts. They were cheaper than the longs and long rifles, and I was finally able to shoot my .22 rifle. It was good.

It also wasn't very accurate. After several shots, I was finally able to at least hit the paper. But I was rapidly going through the limited amount of ammo I had. The homemade sights worked, and after a lot of careful adjustment with pliers and a file, I was able to even hit my target. By now, it was obvious to my dad that I was serious about hunting with this rifle, so he took it to a gunsmith and had a real set of sights put on it, and had it sighted in so it would be accurate. Now my .22 was ready to hunt and so was I.

I also carefully sewed together scrap pieces of leather for a gun case so that when not in use, the rifle would be protected from damage. And since the rifle was a single shot, I carefully drilled holes in the butt stock for spare bullets just in case I ever found myself in the middle of a big hunt and ran short of ammo I'd have a few rounds in reserve. I made the butt plate out of a piece of flat plastic. It covered the spare bullets and protected them. In order to properly display my rifle, and thus have it readily accessible and at the same time keep it out of reach of my siblings, I made a gun rack for the wall. I made it in my shop class at school and intentionally made it large enough to hold three rifles to allow room for additional fine rifles. I was real proud of that little rifle.

I practiced shooting every chance I had and every time I could afford a box of ammo. And I got real good with the little rifle. I learned its limits, and it was deadly as long as I didn't exceed those limits. It was fun to shoot and was all I needed. The fact that it was a single shot rifle required me to make every first shot count. This was especially important considering that my cousin had a .22 with a magazine and a neighbor had one that was a semiautomatic with a tubular magazine. I could hold my own with that little .22 rifle.

I still have that little .22 rifle, and even though it hasn't been fired in a few years, it occupies a prominent position in my gun safe. I can't begin to tell you how many squirrels, rabbits, and other critters it dispatched over the years. I can tell you that I'm not ready to part with it yet, but when I do, I'll probably give it to my son, B. J. He has already expressed a desire to have it. He could do worse. The fact that he was named after my dad adds to that decision. We'll just keep it in the family and hand it down to the next generation. Who knows, maybe he'll have a son someday.

Squirrel Tales to Game Trails And Shore Lunches

2 Squirrels, Rabbits, and Ducks

Where I grew up in Michigan, we lived halfway down a two-mile long gravel road that was a dusty, potholed washboard in the summer, a frozen potholed washboard in the winter, and a muddy potholed washboard the rest of the year. We had woods all around us except for where neighbors had cleared enough area for a house and yard. Our nearest neighbor to the east was a mile away. We had neighbors across the road and to the west all the way to the end of the road. We had no one behind us for two miles, and there was a creek between us at that. We had a lot of room to run and play. Since we were such a large family, and we lived in a very small, four-room house, counting the basement, if the weather was at least dry, we were playing outside. To this day, I'd rather be outdoors than in. I just have to get outside every day and "get a little bit of it on me."

Coming from such a large family, we naturally each had chores to do. As I mentioned earlier, beginning at age thirteen, when I got home from school, I went to the garage

6   Squirrels, Rabbits, and Ducks

to help my dad. Between school, homework, and helping my dad in the garage and around the junkyard, and other activities such as band, sports, and sleeping, I didn't have a lot of time to do much hunting. Fortunately, with all the woods around us, I didn't have far to go when I did get a chance. I could walk out the back door and be in the woods. And I did this every chance I got. I miss that, and long for the ability to do that again. Maybe someday.

Don't get me wrong, though, we never hunted or fished out of season. At the time, you didn't need a license to hunt small game in Michigan if you were under sixteen and hunting on your own property. We also obeyed the old rule of only taking rabbits in months with an "r" in them, so we were safe when the season fell in those months. By the time I turned sixteen, I was working regularly enough to afford a hunting license and hunt on property other than our own. It was good.

Do you remember the first hunt you went on and what you hunted? Do you remember the first animal you shot? Do you remember how the hunt unfolded and those feelings as you admired your first quarry? Do you remember where you were, whom you were with, and what the weather was like? Was it what you expected it to be?

I remember mine like it was yesterday. I also hope that I never forget it, either. For a fourteen-year-old kid who thought he wanted to hunt living animals, "the first" would determine if there would be a second. As it was, it turned out to be everything I thought it would be and so much more. It was my rite of passage to a sport that I still enjoy to this day. The day I no longer look forward to my next hunt and get excited when the day arrives, I will know it is time for me to stop hunting.

Okay, picture this: It was one of those picture perfect fall days in a Michigan September. I got off the school bus and

Squirrels, Rabbits, and Ducks

hurried into the house to change my clothes. I told my mom that I'd like to go out in the woods behind the house to hunt squirrels for a little while, and that I wouldn't go too far or be gone too long. She said okay. I grabbed my .22 and a handful of ammo and headed for the woods behind our junkyard. Being quite familiar with these woods, I had a pretty good idea where I wanted to sit in hopes of getting a shot at a big fat fox squirrel. With several squirrel nests in the area and lots of acorns, I just knew this would be the day.

I quietly made my way through the undergrowth and brush to a huge oak tree that had a large squirrel nest in it. From the base of this tree, I could see at least three other squirrel nests in the area. I decided to give this spot a try and made myself as comfortable as I could on the ground at the base of the tree in the shade.

As I sat there quietly waiting for the woods to get quiet again, I couldn't help but notice how it was warm in the sun and very comfortable in the shade. The leaves were already turning colors and beginning to fall. Even so, the trees provided a thick canopy overhead and offered ample cover for squirrels and birds trying to figure out why I had invaded their privacy. Soon these trees would be bare, and the whole area would take on a distinctly different beauty under a blanket of snow.

I was less than two hundred yards from the house, yet it may as well have been two hundred miles. Even though I could still hear voices at the house, I could shut them out and hear birds and wind and squirrels. By concentrating hard on noises and movement, I had hopes of seeing the squirrel before he saw me. If I were lucky, he'd never know I was there. If not, I would have to try some of the tricks of the trade.

On the other hand, I knew that the squirrel was well-attuned

8   Squirrels, Rabbits, and Ducks

to sounds and movement, and therefore, it was even more important that I remain still and keep as quiet as possible. If I had any hope of taking a squirrel, I would have to beat him at his own game and on his home turf. I would have to outsmart him by out waiting or ambushing him. I knew I could do it, and I'd keep trying until I did.

I didn't have long to wait. I had only been settled into my spot for half an hour or so when I caught movement on the ground in front of me. It was a large fox squirrel and he was coming straight at me. He was probably thirty yards away when I first saw him, and now that I knew he was there, I could hear every movement he made in the dry leaves. He didn't know I was there, but if I moved, he would. Now what do I do? I thought.

At about fifteen yards, I got the break I needed. He stopped, sat straight up, and took a long look at me. He then began to chew me out for being in his woods. I don't know what he said, but I could tell by the tone of his voice that it wasn't nice. I don't believe I could have printed it here if I did know what he said. He was mad.

At this point, I began to wonder if I shouldn't just get up and leave. I wondered if my .22 was going to be enough to cleanly dispatch this very irritated squirrel. Should I apologize? What if I shot and only wounded him? Did I have enough bullets to finish him off? Do wounded squirrels attack? I had a hundred other questions.

I decided to go for it. I had come this far, I had waited for this day, and I was ready. I slowly raised my .22 and took careful aim. The squirrel seemed to stand there in defiance. I couldn't believe it. He just stood there and called me every name in the squirrel book of bad names. Now I was more determined than ever to pull the trigger. No squirrel was going to talk to me like that and get away with it. I certainly didn't want him to brag to all his friends how he had faced

Squirrels, Rabbits, and Ducks

down a hunter, and it was me.

I carefully released the safety with my thumb, made sure it was still a good open shot, lined up the sights, and squeezed the trigger. I don't remember even hearing the sound of the rifle firing. Since it was a .22 rifle, there was no recoil. Yet, when I looked at where the squirrel had been, I couldn't see him.

My heart sank. I just knew I had missed. I jumped to my feet and ran to where the squirrel had last been standing. Now I started questioning myself again. Why did I shoot? I hoped he wasn't wounded and crawled off to die a slow, painful death, because I wanted to be a hunter. I began having second thoughts about ever shooting at a living animal again.

I couldn't believe my eyes. When I got to the spot, there he was, lying in the leaves, dead. The bullet had hit him exactly where I had aimed. I had made my first kill and I was shaking all over. I also had an urge to pee. I didn't remember having the urge before that, but right then, I had to put my rifle down and take care of this pressing business.

With that taken care of, I picked the squirrel up and looked him over real good. I was proud, yet sad, with what I had done. All I could think of next was taking the squirrel home and cleaning it, something I had never done before. But first, I had to show it to my mom and anyone else who wanted to see it. Mom was very pleased for me and quite excited, and from that day on, was always anxious to hear about my hunts, both successful and unsuccessful. I miss her.

Being my first squirrel, I naturally wanted to keep the pelt and tail. This meant carefully skinning the animal so that I could salt the hide and tail to preserve them. It was hard enough to do it by myself, having never skinned one before, but I also had an audience of younger brothers to watch me. I was under a lot of pressure, and the stress was almost more

10   Squirrels, Rabbits, and Ducks

than I could handle. Almost.

After about an hour of "wrestling" with an already dead squirrel, I had succeeded in removing the hide and tail, the head, and all four paws. Now came the tricky (and messy) part. Nothing to it. I opened that squirrel up with the precision of a brain surgeon. After removing all the innards, I washed it off with lots of fresh water and then quartered the carcass. It was at that point that I realized that it was going to take a lot more than one squirrel to feed our family. I was going to have to shoot a lot more if I hoped to have enough for all of us. I had my work cut out for me and I knew what I had to do. I was up to the task and hooked on hunting. That little .22 rifle would account for many more squirrels over the years, and even though it doesn't get much use anymore, I'm confident it is still up to the task.

I have another .22 rifle that I like to shoot just for the fun of it because it's economical to shoot and very accurate. I have, over the years, taken a few squirrels, rabbits, and even an odd quail or two with it. It's a Marlin, bolt action, seven shot, magazine-fed rifle that I bought new many years ago. Before I even shot it, I reshaped and refinished the stock, and mounted a little four-power .22 rifle scope on it. It shot well, but not great, so I replaced that 4x scope with a 4x riflescope with a one-inch tube. Now it shoots great. Once again, though, I know this rifle's limits, and it is deadly as long as I stay within them.

Anyway…

I don't remember the first rabbit I shot. It could have been a cottontail in our backyard, or a cottontail I caught alive in our backyard in a homemade live trap. I just don't remember anymore. But I do remember more than a few rabbits going in the freezer as a result of my hunting. Together with the squirrels, those rabbits provided meals that helped reduce the food bills for our large family. And like my mom always

Squirrels, Rabbits, and Ducks

told us, you eat what she prepared or you go hungry. She was a great cook, and managed to make squirrel and rabbit taste real good to hungry kids.

And did I mention ducks? Let me tell you about how we hunted ducks back then. Please note that I said hunted, and not shot, ducks. There is a distinct difference, and it's not for lack of trying, but we never did get a duck with our .22 rifles. Also notice that I said we. Enter my cousin, the one with the .22 rifle with a magazine. He was six months younger than me and lived about a quarter mile down the road from us.

After I got my .22 rifle from my dad, his dad bought him a new one. Now I had a hunting partner. Whenever we went exploring in the woods, one or both of us had our .22 rifles with us, just in case. Since I was always short on shorts (bullets), my cousin was usually the one with the rifle. Not a good idea. He would shoot at anything. Fortunately, he wasn't a good shot, so he didn't hit anything very often.

It was during one of our many expeditions into the woods behind our houses that we noticed a few ducks in the creek, and more in the ponds along it. Well, you can guess what that meant. We decided that we had to try to get close enough to the ducks to shoot one. This turned out to be a lot more difficult than we anticipated. Duck hunting with .22 rifles proved to be quite a challenge, but we were up to it.

After numerous failed attempts to sneak up on these ponds and ambush an unsuspecting duck before it could fly away, we pulled out all the stops. It was now an obsession with us and we were more determined than ever to get a duck, even if it was the last thing we ever did. We were driven to succeed. We were confident. We were lucky we didn't shoot any, because they were not in season, we didn't have a license or a duck stamp, and we didn't have a clue what kind of duck we were looking at, in most cases. And

12 Squirrels, Rabbits, and Ducks

it wasn't the last thing we ever did either, thank goodness.

We soon realized that if we hoped to get a shot at a duck, we would have to find a way to get in range without disturbing them. Obviously, our sneaking skills left a lot to be desired. We first cleared a trail that we could use to get into position. Then we built a natural brush blind overlooking the pond, and practiced getting into it as quietly as possible. We were ready. But the ducks didn't cooperate. They moved on to another pond and remained out of range. What to do now?

Not to be outsmarted by ducks, we (I) made a decoy. I mean, why not, huh? If I can make sights for my rifle, I can make a duck decoy, too, right? Right. Just how difficult can it be, huh? After all, you just nail some wood together, carve it to shape, and you have a decoy, right? Wrong.

My decoy had a fairly square-shaped body because I used scrap pieces of used 2x4s for the body, and I got real tired of trying to carve it to shape, real fast. The head didn't look too bad, and the natural wood color made it look like a female duck to me. I was convinced that it was good enough to fool a duck.

Knowing virtually nothing about duck hunting or decoys, I had overlooked a few minor details. It wasn't until my cousin and I took it down to the creek and put it in the water that we realized that it listed to one side when it floated. So we went back to the garage to insert a weight in the bottom. Then back to the creek to put it out. It immediately drifted into the weeds. We went back to the garage to attach an anchor, and then back to the creek to put it out again. It didn't work. Back once more to the garage to paint it, and then back to the creek. It still didn't work. The only thing we got for all our efforts was a lot of exercise running back and forth between the garage and the creek. The ducks weren't impressed or fooled.

Even though we never did succeed in shooting a duck,

Squirrels, Rabbits, and Ducks

and it obviously wasn't the last thing we ever did, we did succeed in bothering or disturbing those ducks enough that they finally moved on south for the winter. The creek is still there, but the whole area is now private property, and the ponds and creek are no longer accessible to exploration by boys with an interest in hunting. A landfill covers the area where we tried to ambush ducks, and I've been told the creek is so polluted that it is "dead." Ducks probably don't land there anymore, anyway. What a shame.

Years later, someone came across a homemade duck decoy in the garage, and Mom told the story of how hard I had worked to make it. Everyone had a good laugh, including me, when she told me about it. I miss her.

My hunting-partner cousin has also since passed away. I miss him, too.

No one knows what happened to the decoy.

Squirrel Tales to Game Trails And Shore Lunches

3   My First Shotgun

After our futile attempts to hunt ducks with .22 rifles, I realized that I would stand a better chance of success if I had a shotgun. I would have to convince my dad that I really needed a shotgun, and I knew that was not going to be easy to do. I was now sixteen years old and regularly working a part-time job after school, so I had a few dollars saved up. I just needed to press the issue with him.

Even though he wasn't very enthusiastic about my wanting a shotgun, he never did say no, or yes. So, when I brought home a bargain shotgun, what could he say? He said a lot, and most of it was loud. He was very disappointed that I had to have another gun. It didn't matter that it was a shotgun. It was another gun. We talked at length about it, and I still have that shotgun. I miss him.

That bargain shotgun was a Mossberg 16 gauge, bolt action, three-shot magazine with an adjustable choke. It had been advertised in the newspaper want ads, so I went to look at it. It was at a used car lot, and the dealer had taken it as a deposit on a car. He wanted twenty dollars for it. After I looked it over good, I bought it from him. As I drove away, I couldn't help but wonder what kind of car he had given in trade. I also thought it ironic that both my guns had been acquired through a car related transaction. Was it an omen?

Like my .22 rifle, this gun was well used, but in much better condition. It had been cleaned, it wasn't covered in rust, and it had the front sight intact. It also just "felt good," so I knew it would be good. It felt good to hold it, to carry it, and when I shouldered it, it fit just right. Do you know what I mean? Like my .22 rifle, I refinished the stock and cleaned it up good before I ever fired it. It was beautiful, and it was mine.

I have had a couple of other shotguns over the years since then, and I sold one of them that I bought new. It was also a Mossberg, but it just didn't fit right when I shouldered it. When I sold it, it had not seen a box of shells go through it. I should not have bought it in the first place. Since then, whenever I look at a gun, be it a pistol, rifle, or shotgun, if it doesn't fit or feel right, I put it back. I don't care how pretty the wood is or how much it costs, it's not worth it to me if it doesn't fit or feel right to me. I bought all my guns to hunt with, not just to look at. After all, you don't buy a good pair of boots for looks alone, do you? If they don't fit properly and feel good, you won't wear them, or they'll be uncomfortable when you do. The same holds true for a gun, only worse, in that a poor fit will most likely also affect your aim. It's one thing to walk funny because your feet hurt, but it's not funny when you don't shoot straight because your weapon doesn't fit you correctly.

Now that I had a shotgun I needed to practice with it if I ever hoped to shoot anything on the wing. This was the one area I had failed to take into consideration when I decided I needed a shotgun. Not the wing shooting, but the practice.

My First Shotgun

The cost of my shooting just went up, big time. Where I was spending less than a penny a shot with my .22 rifle, I was spending over twenty cents a shot with my shotgun. Every five shots with my shotgun were worth one hundred shots with my .22. It was obvious to me that I couldn't afford to practice with my shotgun very often, or I better become a good shot real fast.

Remember my two friends in high school who liked to hunt and fish, and who introduced me to hunting and fishing? Well, one of them also reloaded their ammo, including for their shotguns. This was good. Even though it was still pretty expensive, I was able to practice a little more often using reloads. I supplied the materials and my labor, and used their equipment. They always helped ensure that I didn't do anything stupid, like blow their place up. What I saved reloading I spent on clay pigeons. I learned quickly that clay pigeons are one-time use only if you hit them. Until I got better at hitting them, I was able to use most of them more than once.

I never was able to practice enough to become real good with that shotgun. When I missed a shot, I knew it was my fault. The gun itself never let me down. This was always the case when it came to wing shooting ducks, woodcock, partridge, or pheasants, and was also true when I missed a running cottontail or snowshoe rabbit. Too many times I didn't "lead" the animal correctly, or it was out of range.

Just like with my .22 rifle, once I learned the limits of my shotgun and recognized my own limitations, I began to hit once in a while what I shot at. But until then, all I was doing was scattering lead shot in the general direction of whatever it was that I was shooting at. For the most part, those animals didn't have anything to worry about when I shot at them.

I had never considered using my shotgun for hunting

anything other than birds and rabbits until one day, while roaming the woods with my .22 rifle, I came across another hunter who was also hunting squirrels. However, this guy had a dog to help tree the squirrels, and he was using a shotgun to shoot them. He also had a couple of squirrels in the bag already as proof that his system worked better than mine did. After tagging along with this guy for a couple of hours, I was amazed at how well his system worked.

The key to his success was the dog. It never missed. If it said there was a squirrel in a tree, you could bet there was. It would stand at the tree and bark until we arrived, and was impatient if we didn't get a squirrel quick enough. Once the squirrel was in the bag, he would head off after another one.

I don't remember what kind of shotgun this guy used, but it was a .410 gauge, and it was quite effective. He shot squirrels in the trees and they fell to the ground dead. He also shot into a squirrel nest and a squirrel came out and fell to the ground dead. In another case, he shot into a squirrel nest and ended up climbing the tree to get the squirrel out of the nest. He said that didn't happen very often, but it bothered me that it happened at all. I wondered how many he lost that way.

After that experience, I decided the shotgun was my best all-around gun for hunting small game, so I carried it whenever I went into the woods. Then one day I shot a squirrel with it. After cleaning the squirrel and seeing the damage, I decided I would continue to hunt them with my .22 rifle. After finding a few pieces of lead shot in the meat while eating it, I was even more convinced to use the .22 rifle. And besides, it was cheaper to shoot, too.

As for those ducks, the reason I needed a shotgun in the first place, I never did so much as even take a shot at them. Oh, I tried, but they must have figured out that I was serious about shooting them and moved to safer places. Between

My First Shotgun

the brush blind, the homemade decoy, and the shotgun, I can't help but believe the odds were in my favor and that it was just a matter of time before I would have succeeded in getting a duck.

In closing this chapter, let me say that I have kept my promise and have not shot another squirrel with a shotgun. I still prefer to use a .22 rifle with a scope. As for ducks, I have since managed to take a few ducks with a shotgun over the years, but only a few, maybe four or five. And I have to tell you that, in my opinion, duck hunting, and for that matter goose hunting and even dove hunting, are overrated. More on that later, but in my case, I wasn't impressed by the taste of the ducks, geese, or doves. They were all too strong tasting for me, and I just can't bring myself to shoot anything I'm not going to use.

I have been known to hunt doves in Texas in September numerous times with one of my brothers and some of our friends. I always use my 16 gauge, bolt action because I am a much better shot with it. It shoulders every time right and it fits against my cheek so that my line of sight is right down the barrel. There is no effort in aiming at that point. It's just a matter of lead, safety off, and fire, all in one smooth motion. Between being good on the first shot, and the fact that it's a bolt action, I am successful and don't waste a lot of shots in the process.

The doves we shoot don't go to waste, either. My brother happens to like them, so I give my birds to him. Since only the dove's breast is eaten, they are quick and easy to clean. Even so, as far as I'm concerned, if you need to soak the breast over night in milk, stuff it with a jalapeno pepper, wrap it in bacon, and grill it over mesquite wood to make it taste good, I'm not interested. It still tastes like liver to me.

So for all you avid dove hunters, go for it, shoot straight, good luck, and enjoy your meals of dove. Just remember to watch out for the rattlesnakes.

I also want to say that one of my two high school friends that helped introduce me to hunting and fishing, the one that had the reloader, has since passed away. Thank you, my friend, for the memories, and may we hunt together again someday.

Squirrel Tales to Game Trails And Shore Lunches

4 Bird Hunting and Turkeys (With a Shotgun)

For the truly observant of you reading this book, I'm sure you are asking yourself why I chose this title for this chapter. I mean, after all, isn't a turkey a bird? Yes, it is. But for those of us who have hunted wild turkeys, we know that they are not just another bird. Unlike their domestic cousins, the wild turkey is not stupid. It is very capable of embarrassing even the most accomplished turkey hunter, and has done so on more than one occasion. You fellow turkey hunters know what I mean. I'll go further into my wild turkey hunting experiences and observations later in this chapter.

I do want to touch briefly on some of my experiences hunting, specifically, various types of birds. That was the reason I needed a shotgun in the first place remember? I have been fortunate to have had the opportunity to hunt

22   Bird Hunting and Turkeys (With a Shotgun)

birds over the years, but I have to admit that I never really enjoyed, or got hooked on, any kind of bird hunting except for wild turkeys, and we haven't got to that part of this chapter, yet. I'll tell you when we get there, but I'm sure you'll recognize it.

I used the word fortunate because I believe that to be the case. I've hunted partridge, woodcock, pheasants, prairie chickens, quail, doves, ducks, and geese, and have been successful in each case. I've been more successful in some cases than in others, though. Case in point, ducks. Even so, I can't brag about my hunting prowess with birds in any case. I'm just not a big bird hunter. No reflection on those who are, I'm just not one of them.

Where I grew up in Michigan there were a few partridges, fewer woodcock, almost no pheasants, no prairie chickens or quail, and what doves there were, we didn't hunt. You already know all about my early duck hunting experiences and I never did any goose hunting up there. I didn't hunt doves, quail, geese, or ducks again until I moved to Texas many years later. I hunted prairie chickens and pheasants in Kansas.

I do remember many days of tromping through the woods behind our house in Michigan hunting small game. Once I turned sixteen, I had to buy a hunting license. If you hunted deer, it required a separate license. Small game was considered squirrels, rabbits, woodcock, and partridge.

Small game season, if I remember correctly, usually opened in September and closed by the end of December. In Michigan, that meant hunting conditions could be beautiful fall days, rainy cool days, or cold and snowy days. It didn't matter to me what the weather was like, I hunted every chance I got. I hunted according to the conditions. At least I was outside, and I was doing what I loved to do.

I used to prefer a damp, drizzly day to hunt partridges

Bird Hunting and Turkeys (With a Shotgun)

because the rain would tend to hold them in the pines. I'd slip quietly and slowly through the pines, carefully watching for the partridge, only to have one or more bust cover and just scare the heck out of me. This would generally result in no shot as I tried to recover my composure, or at best, a hasty shot at a bird that was usually out of range by the time I could react. I did "connect" on a couple of occasions, but I have to admit it was more luck than skill when I did.

Another good time to hunt partridge was immediately after a heavy snowfall. On more than one occasion I was able to literally "boot" a partridge out from under a blanket of new snow and connect as he flew off. The reason I say "boot" a partridge out is because in several cases, the partridge didn't want to flush out of the snow until I booted it out with my foot. Once again, I would very carefully work the edge of the pines looking for a peephole in the snow. This is a hole no larger than a quarter where the partridge breathes through. By staying ready while moving closer to the peephole, I would get off a shot as the partridge burst out of the snow and flew away.

If you have ever hunted woodcock, you know how hard they are to hit. When they did flush, it was always a surprise as they zigzagged around trees while flying very fast for distances just out of shotgun range. Once again, I had a tendency to spread lead shot in the general area of the bird, only to shoot where the bird had been a split second earlier instead of where it would be when the shot got there. (I missed a lot.) I do remember getting one once, but like squirrels, soon realized it would take a lot of woodcocks to feed our family even one meal. I don't remember how it tasted.

The sum total of my pheasant and prairie chicken hunting consisted of a single weekend hunt with some friends a few years ago in Kansas. We had a great time and even got a few birds. I can see how hunting pheasants and prairie chickens

24   Bird Hunting and Turkeys (With a Shotgun)

could be addictive. Plus, it only takes a few birds for a nice meal. I look forward to doing more pheasant and prairie chicken hunting in the future, the Good Lord willing.

After moving to Texas many years ago, I had the opportunity to hunt doves, quail, ducks, geese, and wild turkeys. Now, as you know, Labor Day is a national holiday. However, in Texas, it's much bigger than that. Dove season always opens on Labor Day and is very popular. In fact, it's almost a "holy day of obligation" for all Texas hunters. It happens to be the beginning of hunting season, and serves to get avid die-hard hunters in the mood for deer season that opens a month later.

It also happens to still be summer in Texas, and in my opinion, too dang hot to be sitting around sunflower fields and stock tanks waiting for doves to fly by. Temperatures are still crowding one hundred degrees, are routinely in the 90s, and rarely drop below 80 in September, even at night. And to top it off, the best time to hunt doves is in the early afternoon during the peak heat of the day when the doves go to water before they roost for the night. All this for the breast only and it tastes like liver to me. I can't stand the taste of liver. Not really my idea of fun. I'm telling you, "You got to love it." This brings a whole new meaning to "being out in the sun too long."

Having hunted doves a few times, and because of the time of year and the fact that I don't care to eat the meat, I probably won't hunt them again. Add to that the matter of not being able to hit them with any regularity, and you can understand why I don't get very excited about dove hunting. I do recognize dove season as the harbinger of bigger and better things to come, and start anticipating the fall deer and turkey seasons only two months away. I am not in any way being critical of the hunters that do enjoy dove hunting. I just think they have been out in the sun too long.

Bird Hunting and Turkeys (With a Shotgun) 25

Quail hunting in Texas is also very popular and can be a lot of fun if you hunt with dogs. They point the coveys of birds and even retrieve them after they are down. The season runs later in the fall when the days are cooler, which also makes it more enjoyable. I don't know anyone who has dogs, and I don't have any of my own, so I haven't done much quail hunting. I do enjoy a good meal of quail, but once again, it takes quite a few to make a good meal. You can figure on at least two per person, and even at that, you better plan on all the fixings, including desert, if you want to come away from the table feeling full.

I think it's only appropriate, at this point, to fill you in on another significant reason why I don't get too excited about dove hunting, or even quail hunting. Rattlesnakes. Do I need to say more? They tend to live in the same areas that we hunt dove and quail. I'm not an expert on snakes, I don't like snakes, and I try very hard to avoid snakes if at all possible. When I do come across a snake, I don't hang around long enough to try to identify it. To me, they are all "rattle-headed copper moccasins" and should be left alone to do their thing. Most of the guys I hunt with feel the same way.

One time I was with a friend coming off our deer lease in central Texas when he spotted a large, black snake under a calf feeder. He stopped his truck, loaded his deer rifle, and shot the snake out the driver's window. He shot it many times, reloaded, and shot it some more. He then put the rifle down, said how much he hated snakes, and we drove away. I was impressed with his shooting skills because we must have been thirty yards away from the snake when he opened fire on it. But enough about snakes. I get chills just thinking about them.

As for ducks and goose hunting, I've noticed that the seasons happen to fall during the wettest, coolest, windiest, most miserable time of the year, and usually requires one to get out in the most miserable conditions. We also don't hunt them except in the mornings, so that they have all afternoon and evening to laugh at how bad a shot we are. Actually, I'm told it gives them a chance to relax and get a good night's sleep before they have to dodge our shot again the next morning. I don't know about you, but to me, I would think that if they were good and tired, we would have a better chance of hitting them. What do you think? I think we're on to something here.

I can't believe that we can be so considerate of ducks and geese while subjecting ourselves to such abuse and discomfort. You really "got to love it" to be a duck or goose hunter or you have to be a glutton for punishment. Who knows, maybe they have been out in the cold too long. What's even more mind-boggling to me is that I have never eaten a wild duck or goose that really tasted good. They were all gamey tasting, with some tasting more like the fish and mud they live on. And then you have the problem of pieces of shot in the meat. No, I'm not a real fan of duck or goose hunting, and probably won't do it too many more times. As much as I love the outdoors, I have better things to do, especially at O-dark thirty in the morning. Lying in cold, wet rice paddies in the dark isn't my idea of fun. I prefer to be warm, dry, and sleeping at that time of the day.

Based upon my comments up to this point, it's probably very obvious to you that wearing out shotgun barrels on my shotguns is not a major concern to me as far as bird hunting goes. I've never had the time or money to shoot much trap, skeet, clay pigeons, or sporting clays, so I probably won't wear shotgun barrels out that way, either. Looking back on it now, why did I need a shotgun anyway? Worse yet, three of them. Oh well, they all "fit" and feel right when I do hunt with them. Besides, just like rifles, you can't ever find one that does everything you want to do with it, so you really do need more than one, right? How's that for logic? How's that for making a case for another shotgun or rifle?

Bird Hunting and Turkeys (With a Shotgun) 27

GOBBA-GOBBA-GOBBA-GOBBLE!!!!

Did you hear that? What was that? Did you recognize it? We're here. It's time to talk a little turkey. I know there are hundreds of "how to" books out there on turkey hunting, and at least that many so-called, or self-professed, experts on the subject. I've read a lot of those books, and magazine articles, watched the videos, listened to the tapes, bought the calls, and talked a lot of turkey with fellow hunters and more than a few turkeys. And I'm here to tell you that I don't claim to be an authority on turkey hunting, but I am hooked on it.

It all happened innocently enough when I shot at my first wild turkey. Please note that I said "shot at." It was many years ago as I was sitting in the hill country of Texas, minding my own business, and trying to do a little deer hunting. I remember it as if it happened yesterday. It was the first time a wild turkey would outsmart me, and it wasn't the last time.

It was one of those warm, lazy days in the fall and I was sitting under a tree, half asleep, just enjoying being alive and taking in a large dose of Mother Nature at her best. All was right with the world around me, and I was at peace. Then it happened. All of a sudden, out of nowhere, there were a number of large black objects moving along a fence line about a hundred yards away. Where did they come from? What were they? What do I do now?

After taking a good look at them through my binoculars, I figured out that they were wild turkeys, and not turkey buzzards. I also decided that if I was going to shoot one, I should probably try before they wandered off. They were in season, I had the appropriate tags, and I was shaking so much that I didn't stand a chance of hitting one of them. But I had to try.

Now remember, I'm hunting deer at the time all this is

28   Bird Hunting and Turkeys (With a Shotgun)

happening, so I have a deer rifle with me, not a shotgun. But then the turkeys are at least a hundred yards away so a shotgun would not have done me any good, anyway. Since I'm using a rifle, I decide that I'll shoot for the head so I don't waste any meat. So I pick out a turkey with a beard, knowing that it is either a tom (male) or a bearded hen, both of which were legal at the time. I put the crosshairs of my scope on its head and realize that I'm shaking so bad that if this works, it'll be by pure luck. Then, to make matters worse, the turkey won't stand still, either. Even when he did stop walking, his head never stopped bobbing around long enough to get a shot off. All I can hope for is that, when I shoot, the turkey will walk in front of my bullet. I had to try. I had nothing to lose and everything to gain.

I shot. I didn't even hear the shot, but I felt the recoil. I quickly put my rifle down and stared in amazement as at least thirty turkeys flew and ran in all directions. They went everywhere, and they didn't waste any time getting there. In just a few seconds, there wasn't a turkey to be seen in the area, including dead ones. I had missed. So much for luck.

After checking to make sure that I had not wounded the turkey, I went back to the tree I had been sitting under to analyze what had just happened. After careful consideration, I realized that I had learned a couple of valuable lessons about turkey hunting. First of all, turkeys are sneaky. Secondly, they can fly and run fast. And finally, I probably shouldn't shoot for their head with a deer rifle. I decided that the next time I got a shot at a turkey, the results would be different. I would shoot for the big part.

Sometime after that, a year or so later, the opportunity presented itself again. As before, I was hunting deer, and therefore I was carrying a deer rifle. This time I didn't give it a second thought. I picked out a legal turkey, put the crosshairs of my scope on its body and fired. The turkey collapsed. The rest scattered just like before. Then one

Bird Hunting and Turkeys (With a Shotgun)

stopped, and I checked to make sure it was a legal turkey. It was, so I shot it, too. It also collapsed. By now, all the others were well on their way to the surrounding counties. I thought this is too easy. There's nothing to this turkey hunting stuff if you shoot for the big part. Then I went to collect my two turkeys.

I was thrilled. Not only had I just shot my first wild turkey, but a double at that. I was absolutely ecstatic. I tagged both of them and put them in the back of my pickup truck and headed for camp. I would clean them there. I couldn't wait to show them to my fellow hunters and tell them all about it.

It was while I was cleaning these two turkeys that I remembered why I had shot at the head of the first turkey I saw. They were a mess. The rifle bullet tore them up, and I ended up wasting a large amount of meat off each of them. By the time I was done cleaning them, they only remotely resembled a turkey. It was sad. It was then that I decided I would not shoot another wild turkey with a deer rifle, at least not in the big part.

In Texas, we have two turkey seasons. One that runs concurrently with our deer hunting season in the fall, and a spring turkey season that stands alone. In the fall season, we are allowed to shoot toms, jakes (young males), and bearded hens. It's during the fall season, when people are deer hunting, that most people shoot their wild turkeys. Therefore, most turkeys shot in the fall are shot with deer rifles, and are mostly incidental to the deer hunt. Not me. I've been there, done that, and got the T-shirt. I will only shoot turkeys with a shotgun.

During the spring season, only toms are legal, and you better be able to tell the difference between toms and hens. The bearded hens are not legal during the spring turkey season, so just because the turkey has a beard doesn't make it a tom or a legal turkey. It's this season that turkey hunters look forward to the most. It's the time of the year when toms show off for the hens, when breeding occurs, when toms have a tendency to gobble, and may even come to a call made by a hunter. It's a great opportunity to get out in the woods and match wits with a gobbler on his own turf.

The first few years I hunted spring turkeys I was not successful. Try as I may, I could not convince a turkey to come to my call. I was beginning to think that the sounds I made were offensive to the real turkeys. Sometimes I could get a tom to answer. Other times, nothing. Sometimes it sounded like they were close, while at other times it sounded like they were getting further away. Then one year it all came together.

All the conditions were right. I just knew this would be the day. I had slipped quietly into an area above a creek where I had seen turkeys on several occasions. It would be at least thirty minutes before it would start to get light, plenty of time for me to get comfortable and for the woods to forget I was there.

The woods were quiet except for the birds, squirrels, insects, and other local creatures coming to life as the sun rose above the horizon. I had yet to hear the slightest sound of a turkey, so I opted to make the first call. I made the most seductive hen call I knew. When I did, almost immediately a gobbler answered far off in the distance. I called again, and he answered again. This tit-for-tat exchange went on for about an hour with each successive response sounding like he was getting closer. Then he quit answering. For the next two hours or so, I called every fifteen minutes to no avail. I was convinced that he had given up on pursuing romance with this hen I was pretending to be.

I was sitting in some bushes in a wooded area. The natural cover helped to conceal me. I was not using a decoy, so any tom turkey coming to my call would be looking for the hen

Bird Hunting and Turkeys (With a Shotgun)

he heard calling. And that is exactly what happened.

I was hunting with my 16 gauge Mossberg with the choke set at full. I was using #4 shot, and I was confident that if a tom came within thirty yards, he was mine. I was intently concentrating on every movement and sound, but had given up on the turkey that returned my calls earlier. I was also getting tired of sitting there. The spot was no longer very comfortable and it was almost midday. I was sprawled out, staring straight ahead with my shotgun lying across my lap.

Gobba-Gobba-Gobba-Gobba-Gobble!

What the…? All of a sudden, I was totally aware that I had a tom turkey very close to me. Very close. I thought that he was in the bush with me, he was so close. I slowly turned my head to the left and found myself looking at a very large wild turkey approximately five yards away. He was also looking at me now. What to do?

As I sat motionless, I could not help but notice that he stood taller than me where I was sitting. He stood still and tried very hard to figure out where the hen was while I tried very hard to figure out how to get a shot at him. He had come up from behind me on my left side and I never heard him. I finally decided that all I could do was wait for him to make the first move and then I would react accordingly.

After what seemed like several minutes, he turned his head and took several steps away from me. At the same time, I raised my shotgun, aimed at his head, and fired.

He collapsed in place. I had my first spring turkey, and I had done it with my first shotgun. The wait was worth it. While his spirit moved on to the great strutting ground in the sky, his mortal remains went into the freezer and were the centerpiece of our next Thanksgiving dinner. It doesn't get any better than that.

There have been many turkeys since this one taken with a

shotgun. On a couple of occasions, I even managed doubles again. I am still convinced that a shotgun is the best way to take wild turkeys, even though they are limited in range. Know your limit and know theirs. When shot in the head, very few pieces of shot end up in the turkey's body, and you don't ruin or waste any meat.

I had something interesting happen to me while spring turkey hunting one year. I tried using a hen decoy in an area I knew turkeys were frequenting. Twice I was able to call gobblers in, but in both cases, they stalled out about sixty yards out. They refused to come closer and eventually walked off into the brush and out of sight. Sixty yards is too far for me to even attempt a shot, so I got skunked.

What was more interesting was that in the five days I had hunted that season, on three separate occasion's hen turkeys came in to my decoy. The first hen wasn't nice at all, and knocked my decoy over and left. The second hen thumped it a couple times with its wings and then walked away. The third hen didn't hit it, but it got right up in the decoy's face and told it off good. I wish I knew what it said, because it was still carrying on as it walked into the woods. It then flew up into a deadfall, about fifty yards away, and sat there for at least two hours. It finally gave up and flew down from the deadfall, almost as if it was embarrassed and hoping no other turkeys had seen her. It walked into the woods and out of sight.

As for spring turkey hunting with a shotgun, I admit that I am hooked. It's enjoyable, exciting, and happens at a great time of the year. One turkey also feeds a lot of people and it tastes great. I may not wear out a shotgun barrel hunting turkeys, but if the Good Lord is willing, I'll keep trying to.

Squirrel Tales to Game Trails And Shore Lunches

5   My First Deer Rifle

My dad wasn't too surprised when I mentioned deer hunting the first time. By then he knew it was probably going to come up sooner or later. A couple of my uncles, his brothers, hunted deer every fall, and many of the people he worked with did, too.

It was the mid 1960s and deer hunting, or deer season, was very much an important time for many people in Michigan. For a lot of small businesses, it meant income to help see them through the winter months. Some businesses actually shut down during deer season so that their employees could go hunting. Some kids were even excused from school for a week or more so they could join their families in deer camp. Lots of people planned their vacations around deer season. For most of them, deer hunting was a means of filling their freezers with good meat to help them through the year.

I clearly remember one cold Sunday morning, which also happened to be the first day of deer season, that particular year. Mom had gotten us all up, dressed, and ready for church, just as she did every Sunday morning. As we drove into the church parking lot, we were amazed to see a large deer tied across the back of someone's hunting vehicle. This person had succeeded in getting his deer early that morning and, I like to think, was already in church giving thanks. I don't remember what the sermon was about that day, but I'll never forget that scene.

Now that I was an accomplished small game hunter, it only served to pique my interest in big game. In Michigan, that meant whitetail deer. That also meant that I would need a rifle of sufficient caliber to hunt deer with. I would need to get my dad's approval to acquire such a rifle. I would need to determine what rifle I needed, and I would have to find a way to pay for it. Nothing to it, right?

When I asked my dad if it would be all right if I bought a deer rifle and hunted deer, he said yes. He naturally had questions about whom I would hunt with, where, and how I planned to pay for another gun. We both knew that I would be able to hunt with my uncles where they hunted. Since I had yet to select a rifle or caliber, the issue of paying for it could not be addressed. I assured him I would let him know as soon as I did.

When a mail order catalog arrived at the house a few days later, I knew exactly what I was going to do about a deer rifle. In it was an advertisement for military surplus rifles, and the price was right. I could buy a used surplus .303 British Enfield rifle for eighteen dollars. This was back when guns could still be shipped through the mail, and you had to be at least sixteen years old to buy one from the catalog. I was sixteen and I had the eighteen dollars, so I bought my first deer rifle. I also had no idea what I had just bought, but I knew life was good and that I was ready to do some serious big game hunting.

My First Deer Rifle

When the rifle arrived and I unwrapped it, I was amazed at all the wood on it. I did not expect to get a rifle that had wood the full length of the barrel, top and bottom. It had a bayonet lug on the end of the barrel, and tip-up rear peep sights. The stock needed to be refinished, and the rifle in general needed a good cleaning. It was in rough shape, but it had potential. And if I hoped to hunt deer with it that fall, I had a lot of work to do to get it ready. After all, great hunters wouldn't be caught dead in the woods with a rifle in this condition, and being the experienced gunsmith that I was, I was just the person to get this rifle into hunting condition.

The first thing I did was remove all the wood from the barrel and fashion a shortened forearm from the wood on the bottom of the barrel. With some help from my dad, I modified a small hose clamp to attach the front end of the forearm to the barrel, and made a fitting for a front sling attach point at the same location. Next, I cut the end of the barrel off just behind the bayonet lug and modified the long-range rear peep sight to an open sight. After a good cleaning, and refinishing the stock, the rifle was ready to hunt with.

Have you noticed a common thread with each of my first guns? They all needed work when I got them. I was able to customize each of them, to some extent, by refinishing them and modifying features such as sights and forearms, and the end result in each case was a weapon that I had a personal attachment to. I love it.

As it turned out, I had been lucky in that the .303 British was a fairly common deer rifle in Michigan at the time. Ammo was readily available, and even if you ran out, chances were that a fellow hunter was also hunting with a .303 British. After my cousin saw mine, he bought one and hunted with it. He and I hunted our first deer with his dad, and we hunted deer together the first two years. I don't know what happened to his .303, but I still have mine. I not only used it to shoot my first deer and several since then, but

I also used it several years ago to take an elk in Colorado.

I've made some additional changes to that rifle since I started hunting with it. I had a good set of Williams sights put on it, I had the receiver drilled and tapped so I could mount a 3x9 variable power scope on it, and I put a custom Monte Carlo butt stock on it. It's about as customized as I can make it, and it looks great. More importantly, it feels good and it fits.

I hunted moose in Canada several years ago and I carried my .303 British. On several occasions, we met local Indians hunting in the same area. I was surprised to see them hunting with old surplus .303 British rifles. I recognized their rifles, but I don't believe they realized I was also carrying a .303 British. Customized, it looks much different.

A few years ago I read an article about hunting in Australia, and in it the author told how the .303 British is still quite popular down under. He included a picture of a customized .303 British that he used while hunting there, and I swear but for only minor details, his looked like mine. My stock appeared to be much nicer than his, and his still had the bayonet lug on the barrel.

Obviously, I made a good choice when I bought that old .303 British many years ago, huh? Who knows, I may get another chance to hunt big game with it someday. I certainly hope so, the Good Lord willing, of course.

Squirrel Tales to Game Trails And Shore Lunches

6   My First Deer Hunt (and Almost My Last)

If it's possible to overdose on excitement, enthusiasm, anticipation, and confidence, I was there. Now that I had a deer rifle, I couldn't wait for deer season to open. This would be a real test of my hunting skills, a real challenge, and a new milestone in my fledgling hunting career if I succeeded. My mind raced as I tried to plan and prepare for that first deer hunt. I tried not to overlook any details, and as the day drew closer, I found it harder to sleep, and even harder to think about anything else.

Since my cousin and I were both going to be deer hunting for the first time, it was decided that it would be best if we hunted with his dad and another one of our uncles. They didn't have a deer camp or specific location where they hunted regularly, but instead, would hunt several different areas on public land about a hundred miles north of where we lived. This meant that we needed to get up very early and drive approximately two hours before we even got to where we would be hunting. Once there, we would find a place to sit in the dark and wait for daylight. We would then hunt that spot until we either shot a deer or it got dark out. We would then drive back home to spend the night and do it all over again the next day. It was obvious to me that this meant some very long days, but I didn't care. It was going to be great, I just knew it. We would be deer hunting.

I bought my deer hunting license as soon as they went on sale. I was also very quick to apply for a doe permit in hopes that I would increase my chances of putting some venison in the freezer. After all, that was what my primary goal was, even though I was hoping and praying for a buck. When my name was selected to receive a doe permit and it arrived at the house in the mail, I was thrilled. I could taste the venison and knew it was as good as in the freezer. I never doubted I would get a deer, but I didn't think it would take all season, either. How's that for confidence?

I made a list of all the items I would need and identified those that I didn't have already. By this time, my mom was also starting to get pretty excited about my going hunting. She surprised me with a bright orange, insulated zip-up sweater with a hood on it. She was almost as excited as I was.

I had everything I needed put together and ready a week ahead of time. The only thing I was waiting for was opening day to get there, and it seemed like it took forever. Then it was Friday. It was the day before opening day and we finalized all the last minute arrangements. I had to be ready at O-dark thirty in the morning. My two uncles and my cousin would pick me up, and we would be on our way. I couldn't wait. I also couldn't sleep that night.

I was already awake when my mom came to wake me up.

My First Deer Hunt (and Almost My Last)

In fact, I was already dressed and ready to go, except for putting on my shoes and coat. Mom had made me breakfast, packed me a lunch, and made me a thermos of hot chocolate to take with me. It turned out that she couldn't sleep either, and now we were ready. I miss her.

When my uncles and cousin pulled into the drive, we said goodbye and Mom wished us good luck. I put my stuff in the car and we were off. I couldn't believe it. Opening day of deer season had finally arrived and we were on our way. I couldn't wait to get there, to get in the woods, to be deer hunting. It was going to be great. For the next couple of hours, my cousin and I discussed what we would do if... then we were there.

"There" was a two-track road that disappeared into the darkness of the woods in an area we had never been before. Somewhere back "there" we would hunt. It was still dark out, and all of a sudden I got a chill and was shivering almost uncontrollably. The adrenalin had kicked in, big time, and I had that urge to pee. I couldn't sit still and had a great deal of trouble getting my hunting stuff on and getting ready to head into the woods. If I didn't pee real soon, I was going to have a serious problem.

Finally, my uncles decided that we had arrived at where we would hunt that day, and eased the car off the edge of the two-track road. While driving into this point, we had passed several other vehicles pulled off the edge of the road, so we knew we would not be alone in the woods. There would be other hunters in the area, so we reminded each other to know our target before we shot at anything. We also discussed how we would hunt this area so that no one would get lost or hurt. I especially liked that part, and paid particular attention to the not getting lost part.

We got out of the car in the dark, finished getting dressed in our hunting clothes, relieved ourselves, checked our

40   My First Deer Hunt (and Almost My Last)

flashlights, checked our rifles, ammo, lunches, thermos jugs, etc., etc., etc., and did all this without saying a word. We were as quiet as we could be under the circumstances. I'm sure that every deer within a half mile knew we, and all the other hunters in the general area, were there. They had to have.

   I was shivering so badly that to this day I don't know how I was able to stand up. It was finally time to go deer hunting. My uncle whispered to my cousin and me to walk up the two-track road a "couple of hundred yards," and for one of us to walk off the road into the woods on the right hand side "just a little ways" and sit down under a tree and be quiet and sit still. The other one was to do the same thing from that point. That way, we would be separated by a couple of hundred yards, and all we had to do when it was time to come back to the car was walk back to the road, turn left, and follow it back to the car. Simple and brilliant. My two uncles would do the same thing, but they would go back down the road the way we had come in. I had no reason to believe this plan wouldn't work. After all, they were both experienced deer hunters.

   We quietly wished each other "good luck" and started to walk away from the car. I had to stop and relieve myself again, and thought it would be a problem if I needed to pee again once I got in the woods and was trying to hunt. My cousin and I walked off into the darkness with our flashlights lighting our path. I didn't know it could be so dark out. It was pitch black out and without the flashlights, we couldn't see our hands in front of our faces. In just a few minutes, my cousin wished me luck as he disappeared off the road into the woods and darkness. I proceeded on for a few more minutes and did the same. I sat down under a large tree, made myself as comfortable as could be, and decided that at first light I would adjust my position as needed. I needed to pee, again.

My First Deer Hunt (and Almost My Last)

As I sat there, I could not believe how dark it was. Once I turned my flashlight off, I couldn't see my hand in front of my face. I held on to my flashlight for fear of laying it down and not being able to find it again until it got light out. I hoped it would hurry up and get light so that I could see. The longer I sat there, the more noises I heard. The more noises I heard, the more nervous I got. The more nervous I got, the worse I needed to pee. I wished it would get light out.

Eventually, I noticed that I could detect some light and make out the shapes of other trees near me. Within just a few minutes, I could clearly see those trees and could even see the first hint of sunlight in the sky. A few minutes later, I was amazed at how fast the sun rose and I could see again. I was also able to relieve myself again.

As I slowly surveyed my surroundings, I noticed that I was near the edge of a wooded draw and was facing across it. My first thought was that I was glad I had stopped where I did in the dark. It would have been really exciting if I had walked over the edge and into the draw. I also noticed no less than six other hunters clad in red or orange in my immediate viewing area, with one of them less than fifty yards behind me. There was even one that I could see on the other side of the draw. I hoped he knew I was there, too.

I didn't know a lot about deer hunting, but I knew this wasn't a good way to do it. A deer wouldn't stand a chance of survival in this crowd, so I got up and moved further along the edge of the draw to a point where at least I could not see another hunter. I found a spot where I could look down into the draw, so I sat down and waited. I really didn't know what to expect, but I was ready.

By mid morning, I had not yet seen a deer. I had heard a number of shots, and with each one would watch and listen intently with heightened awareness and attention for anything moving, but had not seen anything. Then I heard a distant shot back down the draw in the direction I had come from. Then I heard another and another and another, each one getting closer. I got ready just in case a deer came running through my area. I also wondered if I should have stayed where I was earlier. I might have had a deer if I had only stayed there, I thought. Then I heard another shot, and then someone shot from across the draw. I was ready to get up and leave when I spotted a lone doe running as fast as she could down through the bottom of the draw, and then I realized what all the shooting was about. Everyone on both sides of the draw was shooting at her as she tried desperately to escape. Now it was my turn. I, too, took a shot and missed. I know I missed because I saw the bark fly off the tree I shot fifteen feet in front of me. The doe never missed a stride.

Soon the woods were quiet again, and I wondered if the doe had escaped or if someone had killed her. I wondered how many hunters had shot at her. I wondered if my cousin had shot, and if I had stayed where I was, would I have seen her or maybe even had a better shot at her. I found myself hoping she got safely away after running the gauntlet she went through.

I stayed in that spot until about noon, and then I decided to walk back to the car to eat my lunch. I wanted to make sure that I could find my way back to the car more than anything else. On my way out, I noticed that all the hunters I had seen earlier were gone, and that the woods were quiet and strangely empty. It was an eerie feeling that I had not experienced before. Even the birds were gone. I felt really alone and was relieved when I got to the car.

While I was eating my lunch at the car, my two uncles and my cousin walked up and told me that they had a doe down not too far from the car. I couldn't believe it, so I went with them to retrieve it. I was excited about my uncle shooting a deer and was anxious to hear all the details. As we walked

My First Deer Hunt (and Almost My Last) 43

back to his deer, he told me the whole story.

As it turned out, none of them had seen anything all morning, so they decided to return to the car and have a cup of coffee and an early lunch. It seems that while they were at the car, most of the other hunters in the area also decided to leave the woods for whatever reason. It would also appear that all this hunter movement and activity in the area caused a deer to move about right near the car. My uncle saw it, picked up his rifle, and shot it not a hundred yards from the car. He, along with my other uncle and my cousin, then walked over to it to make sure it was dead and to tag it. It was while they were doing that, and admiring the doe, that I walked up to the car. I had never heard him shoot. I couldn't believe it. I thought, was that all there was to deer hunting, just a case of being in the right place at the right time and pure luck? That's certainly the way it was in this case.

After cleaning the deer, my uncles decided it was time to go home and get the deer hung up to age. We carefully put all our hunting stuff in the car and the deer in the trunk, and headed for home. I couldn't believe we were already on our way home. We had only hunted half a day. When would I get another chance to go again? Is this all there was to it? It was a much quieter trip home.

Even though I was excited for my uncle, I was disappointed for me. We could only individually take one deer a year legally, so my uncle would not be going hunting again that year. My other uncle wasn't as interested in hunting as my cousin and I were, and since my uncle wouldn't be going again that year, neither would he. That left my cousin and me, and we were not experienced enough to go by ourselves. And deer season lasted only two more weeks. I wasn't ready to be done hunting yet, especially after only half a day, and I was desperate to find a way to hunt some more. I could still taste that venison, and couldn't help but think there was

44   My First Deer Hunt (and Almost My Last)

more to hunting than this.

The father and the brothers of my girlfriend at that time also hunted, but they had a place they went to hunt every year. They would take their house trailers and campers up there before the season opened and leave them there until they were done hunting for the season. There was an empty, old, dilapidated house on the property, so they always parked their trailers and campers around it. They had fixed up the living room enough so that it could be used as a "community house" for the camp. A lantern provided the light in the evenings, and a potbellied stove in the center of the room took the chill off. It was an excellent deer camp.

When I explained my dilemma to my girlfriend's father, he invited me to join him and his two sons the next weekend. It was the second weekend of the season and would be the last weekend they would hunt. They had all taken the first week of deer season as vacation and would be going back to work the next Monday. The season would end the following weekend at dark on Sunday, but they would not be able to hunt that weekend. Since I had to go to school during the week anyway, I could only hunt the weekends. With only two weekends remaining, I took him up on his offer. At least I would be deer hunting.

After school that Friday, I drove up north to where their camp was. The directions were very clear and I drove right to it. I arrived in time to spend a few minutes with the rest of the hunters in the community house, and got to meet most of them. Talk was centered on how the hunting had been slow, and how and where everyone would hunt in the morning. It was exciting, and I knew I would have trouble sleeping that night. This was more like what I had hoped it would be. I actually slept quite well.

It was cold in the trailer when we got up. It was also very early. We had a quick cold breakfast and some hot chocolate,

My First Deer Hunt (and Almost My Last)

and went to the community house to finalize our hunting plans for the day. As I stepped out of the trailer, I stepped in about four inches of new snow. Now I knew why it was cold in the trailer. It was good to be alive, and I was excited about being there with other hunters that shared the same excitement. I was shivering all over, and it wasn't because I was cold.

After a brief discussion, everyone knew where he would be hunting. We only had to get our hunting things together and go into the woods to our predetermined locations. We wished each other "good luck" and we headed out. I couldn't stand it any longer. I had to pee.

I had no trouble finding the spot I was supposed to hunt. I made myself comfortable and settled in for a long wait. At lunchtime, one of the other hunters walked up, and together we walked back to camp for lunch. I couldn't help but think how my uncle had shot his deer the weekend before as a direct result of people walking around the woods. When we arrived at the community house, and were warming ourselves around the potbellied stove, I relayed the story to all who were present. No one had seen a deer all morning.

The optimism that everyone had that morning, in anticipation of increased deer activity following the snowfall, was fading fast. Only a couple of hunters had even seen deer tracks. Some had gotten cold and came back to camp early. Others were talking about hunting only until dark and then leaving for home the first thing in the morning. Others who stayed the night were going to hunt the next morning, and then they would head for home about midday. Deer season was rapidly coming to an end for most of these people, and for me, too.

We ate our lunches, got warmed up, and headed back to our spots in the woods. It was a long quiet afternoon. No shots were fired, and no deer were seen. At dark, I returned to camp to find that a couple of the people had already left. They didn't even wait until the next morning like they said they would. It was a much more subdued atmosphere in the community house that evening.

The next morning, a few of us went out and hunted for a couple of hours. When we got back to camp, the others had closed up the community house for another year and were just waiting for us to come in. We put our hunting stuff away, said our goodbyes, and left. The letdown from all the excitement was almost unbearable. Watching everyone leave was very depressing. And then it was quiet. A few tracks in the snow were the only reminders that we had shared a few hours doing what we all loved to do. The next snowfall would erase even that evidence.

As I drove home by myself, I debated whether or not I would ever hunt deer again. To date, my sum total of time spent hunting deer was two days. I wanted to hunt, but I just wasn't sure it was worth it. I liked the camaraderie and being outdoors, but it just wasn't what I had expected. The next weekend would be the last weekend of the season, and once again, I had no place to hunt. It would probably be the next year before I got to go again, if ever. To say the least, I was disappointed. It was a long drive home.

What happened next turned the tide, so to speak. My dad, seeing my determination and desire to hunt, asked a friend of his who he worked with if he knew of some place where my cousin and I could hunt deer and not get in trouble. My dad asked this person specifically because he knew this man was a hunter and fisherman, and may know of an area we could go to, or a person we could talk to, about a place to hunt. As it turned out, his friend had a place to hunt about a three-hour drive north of where we lived and was planning to hunt there the next (and last) weekend of the season, and he invited my cousin and me to join him as his guests. He drew a map of how to find the place and gave it to my dad.

My First Deer Hunt (and Almost My Last)

Needless to say, when my Dad gave us this news, we were ecstatic. I called the man and thanked him, and got further details on what to expect and how to get there. I was thrilled that I would get another chance to do some deer hunting. It would mean another long drive up there in the morning and back home in the evening, but it would be worth it. We were about to experience yet another method of deer hunting.

I was supposed to pick my cousin up at his house at three in the morning so we would have plenty of time to find where we needed to be before it got light out. I was right on time. He was still in bed and asleep when I got there, so he wasn't even ready to leave. I just knew we would be late getting up north and would miss the morning hunting. He hurried up and got ready, we put his stuff in my car, and we were off. He immediately went back to sleep, and slept almost the entire drive up there. Since it was cold out, I had the heater on in my car. After about an hour on the road, my cousin woke up complaining about how his feet were "well done." He had gone to sleep with them in front of the heater. I knew he wasn't as excited about hunting as I was and thought how this could be a long day. The heater did work really well in that car.

It was still dark out when we arrived at the farm where we were to meet my dad's friend. It wouldn't be long before it got light out. Where was everyone? I almost panicked. Were we late (because of my cousin)? Were we at the wrong farm? What do we do now? The house was dark, and there weren't any other cars or trucks there. I couldn't believe we had blown it after all that.

Rather than take a chance and wake someone up in the house, only to find out that we were at the wrong farm, my cousin and I decided to wait at least until we saw some activity in the house before we knocked on the door. We didn't have to wait long. It was only a few minutes before we saw a light on in the house. That was enough evidence for us that someone was up and about and could answer the door. So we knocked on it.

A man answered the door, and after we introduced ourselves and explained what we were doing, and who we were looking for, he said we were at the right place all right, we just happened to be the first to arrive. The others would be arriving any time now. We hadn't blown it after all. We thanked him, went back to my car, got all our hunting stuff ready, and tried to figure out how we could get into the woods before daylight. It would be dawn in less than an hour, and the other hunters hadn't even arrived yet. How do these guys hunt?

As we tried to wait patiently, a car came up the driveway. It was a couple more hunters who had hunted there before, and as we introduced ourselves, another car and a pickup truck arrived with more hunters. Then a couple more cars and another pickup truck pulled in. Even the man who lived there was out in the yard with us, joking and laughing and greeting everyone. There were fourteen hunters by then, and according to the man who owned the place, he thought we were all there. After meeting my dad's friend and introducing ourselves, my cousin and I decided we would stick real close to him and do whatever we were told to do. The rest of the hunters welcomed us and accepted us as one of their group. It was going to be great. I just knew it.

The man who lived there was obviously in charge, and was soon discussing with the rest of us who would be the "dogs" and who would be the "sitters" on the first drive. Drive? The dogs would go with so-and-so in his pickup truck, while the sitters would go with so-and-so in his pickup truck. Each group would be dropped off at specific locations, and at that time the drive would begin. As we got aboard our respective pickup trucks, we asked what we were doing and how it worked. After it was explained to us, it made perfect sense. We would be driving the deer out of areas, and past waiting

My First Deer Hunt (and Almost My Last)

hunters.

Because of the way this property was laid out, it had areas of woods where the deer stayed during the day. Since it was the last weekend of the season, it worked best to hunt these areas in organized drives. Each wooded area would be driven in a specific direction, determined by its size, shape, topography, and access, among other things. We would alternate being dogs or sitters. The dogs would enter and walk-on line from one side of these areas hollering "Hey, you" every so often, while the sitters waited along the sides and opposite end for deer leaving the woods ahead of the dogs. The purpose of hollering "Hey, you" was so that all the hunters knew where the others were so that no one got hurt. See what I mean? It made perfect sense to me.

Two or three drives were made that morning, and then it was time to go back to the farmhouse for lunch. Several hunters had seen deer, but no one had shot a deer during the morning hunt. Several more drives were made that afternoon, and then it was time to head for home. Once again, no one had shot a deer that afternoon. We agreed to meet again in the morning, the last day of the season, and try it again. Several hunters said they would not be back in the morning and said their goodbyes and left. It was questionable if we would have enough hunters to drive the deer in the morning. My cousin and I talked a lot about this method of hunting on our way home. It didn't seem to be very effective.

Early the next morning, I picked my cousin up again and we headed north for one last day of deer hunting for the year. At least this morning he was up and ready to go when I got there. It didn't seem like the drive took as long to get there as it did the day before. We gathered at the farmhouse to plan how and where we would hunt that morning. We only had ten hunters, but we decided to drive the smaller areas anyway. I would start the day as a sitter and my cousin would start out as a dog. We loaded into pickup trucks and headed out. At least we were hunting.

After being dropped off and finding a spot to sit where I could see, I made myself as comfortable as possible. It would probably be between thirty minutes and an hour before the dogs would emerge and the deer would be ahead of them. I wanted to be ready, because we were told the deer are usually on a dead run when they finally bust out of the woods. They were.

I was sitting in front of a stump facing the woods where the dogs were coming through. All of a sudden, a large doe and two yearlings were headed straight at me on a dead run. They were past me and gone before I could get my rifle up. I couldn't believe it. I never had a chance for a shot. Those deer had passed within a few feet of me. I needed to pee.

Then I heard a shot from one of the dogs, so I got ready again in case a deer came running out of the woods. Nothing happened. I sat there for probably another hour before the pickup truck came by to pick me up. When I asked who shot, no one knew in our truck. When we joined the dogs, I found out that my cousin had shot a fox, not a deer. No one else had seen a thing, except for me, and those deer almost ran me over without even getting my gun up, let alone getting off a shot. I felt really bad. I had probably blown my only chance at a deer that year.

We made a couple more drives and then it was time for lunch. I was hungry by then, and so was my cousin. He complained that his stomach was hollering "Hey, you" louder than he was on the last drive. We had our lunch and planned our afternoon hunts. It was a greatly subdued atmosphere, as we all knew we were running out of time to hunt.

This would be it for the season. It was now or not until next year. I was the only one in the group with a doe permit,

My First Deer Hunt (and Almost My Last)

so any deer was legal for me. I was still hoping for a monster buck, but would settle for a doe if I got the chance. It was time to go hunting, and I needed to pee again.

We loaded into the pickup trucks and headed back out. The first two drives were uneventful and produced no opportunities for anyone. We had time for one more drive before it got dark, and it was my turn to be a sitter again. As we spread out just inside the edge of a section of woods, I remember thinking how the season had gone and how it was almost over. I was not very optimistic about my chances of taking a deer that season.

I remember how it had been a bright sunny day, and how the shadows were stretching out for the evening as the sun sank toward the horizon. There was no snow on the ground, but there was a heavy blanket of leaves to insulate the ground from the snows yet to come. The fading sunlight felt good against the promise of a chilly night.

Then I heard a shot off to my right. It had to be another sitter because I had yet to hear any hollering from the dogs. I quickly got ready to shoot in case a deer came through the area I was in. I didn't know what to expect, but I knew that anything moving ahead of the dogs and having been shot at would probably be on a dead run, no matter where it was headed. I was right.

I heard a sitter to my right yell, "They're headed your way," about the same time I saw three deer break into the clearing on a dead run. I didn't see any antlers, but since I had a doe permit, I could shoot either sex. I only had enough time to get my rifle up and aim at the nose of what I perceived to be the largest of the three deer. All three would cross the clearing in front of me, from right to left, and all three were running so fast it looked like their bellies were almost on the ground. This would be my first, and last, real chance to take a deer that season, so I took it.

My First Deer Hunt (and Almost My Last)

I squeezed the trigger and my .303 British recoiled. I don't remember hearing the shot, but I do remember watching the deer I shot at collapse and slide through the leaves until it came to rest at the base of a large tree. The other two deer never slowed down as they disappeared into the woods. Everything was quiet again. It was over just that fast. I had my first deer.

I heard the sitter to my right yell, "Did you get one?"

I yelled, "Yes," and within a few minutes there were a couple of other hunters there to admire my deer and to congratulate me. I was shaking all over again and I wasn't cold. I couldn't stand still. I also needed to pee again.

After we were done talking about what had happened, where the deer had come from, who saw what, and how I had managed to shoot one of them, we field dressed the deer and hung it in a tree to drain and cool while one of the others went to get a truck. It was starting to get dark and cold. My first deer season had just ended successfully, and I was hooked on deer hunting. I couldn't wait for the next season to start. I was ready to do it again. I couldn't wait to show the deer to my mom and dad. Then the truck arrived.

We loaded the deer into the back of the pickup truck and drove to the farmhouse. It was dark when we got there and some of the hunters were ready to leave. After everyone said goodbye and agreed to be back next year, they left. My cousin and I tied my deer across the back of my car and headed home, too. The drive home seemed shorter than the drive up there.

When we got home, my mom and dad, and all my brothers and sisters, had to come out to see my deer. My mom was very happy for me. I then went to my girlfriend's house to show her father. We took a picture of it and then I went back home. I hung the deer in the garage until the next day when I could take it in to be processed at our local grocery store.

My First Deer Hunt (and Almost My Last)

That deer provided quite a few good meals for us over the next few months, and was enjoyed by all. I'll never forget the support and encouragement I got from my mom and dad along the way. I miss them both.

Squirrel Tales to Game Trails And Shore Lunches

7 My Second Deer Hunt

By the time September rolled around again, I was already counting the days until deer season. When I bought my small game license and my deer license, I knew it wouldn't be long. It would be great. After all, I was a seasoned veteran and experienced deer hunter. I knew what to expect, or so I thought.

About a month before the opening weekend of deer season, I got in touch with my dad's friend to confirm that my cousin and I would be able to hunt with them again. A full week before opening weekend, my cousin and I made our final plans to hunt opening day. The anticipation was almost more than I could stand. And then it was opening day. It could have been Christmas Day and my excitement wouldn't have been any higher. That's how it is every opening day for us avid deer hunters. When it stops being like that, I will quit hunting.

Just like the year before, I picked up my cousin early

opening morning, and just like the year before, he wasn't ready. He wasn't even up, let alone ready to go. He hurried up and put his stuff in my car. After we got in the car, he immediately went to sleep. At least he didn't try to broil his feet in front of the heater this time. We were on our way north to hunt whitetail deer, with me driving and my cousin sleeping, just like the year before. I have to admit that he was real good at sleeping in the car.

Along the way, though, I noticed a noise coming from the right front wheel. After stopping to check it out, I determined that the wheel bearing was going out and would need to be repaired before we tried to drive home that evening. Since it was still dark out, and no parts stores would be open for several more hours, I decided to drive on to the farm, hunt the morning hunts, and then see about fixing my car. It turned out to be an excellent decision in more ways than one.

When we arrived at the farm, several other hunters were already there and the excitement of the first hunt of the season filled the air. It was good to be a part of it and share in the excitement. Most of the hunters were people we had met the year before, but there were also a few new faces. After a round of introductions and greetings, and identifying the dogs and the sitters for the first drive, it was time to load into the pickups and head for the woods. I needed to pee.

It was just starting to get light when they dropped us off in the woods. I was a sitter for the first hunt of the season and I wasn't complaining. I walked into the woods and found a spot that looked promising, and made myself comfortable. It was just a matter of waiting for the dogs to start their drive and hope they pushed a deer past me that I could get a shot at. As luck would have it, nature called and I would need to answer her really soon. I waited as long as I could, and then had to take care of business.

I stood my rifle against the tree I had been sitting under

My Second Deer Hunt

and walked over to a bush to relieve myself. I was still putting myself back in order as I walked back to the tree and wasn't paying much attention to anything. When I reached the tree, I picked up my rifle, and before sitting back down, I took a good look all around me. That's when I noticed a four-point buck standing there, looking at me. I was more surprised than he was. Picture this: You're standing up in the open with your rifle in your left hand hanging at your side. There's a buck standing approximately thirty yards away, looking at you. You know that if you move, he's gone, and if you don't move, he will probably be gone soon anyway. What do you do?

Well, being the experienced hunter that I was, I knew that I better keep still until he decided to do something. So that's what I did. I didn't do anything except watch him closely. All I could think about was where did he come from? What do I do now? How am I going to get a shot at him without scaring him off first?

Then he turned his head to look away from me. This was the opportunity I was waiting for. I raised and shouldered my .303 British and took aim at his shoulder. As he turned his head to look back at me, I squeezed the trigger. As usual, I felt the recoil, but didn't remember hearing the shot. As I chambered another round, I looked and the deer was gone. I walked to where he had been standing and found him lying just behind a small rise in the ground. I had my first buck whitetail deer, and as usual, you guessed it, I had to pee.

Having heard the shot, a few of the other hunters came over to see what I had. After the congratulations were done, we field dressed the buck and took it to the farmhouse where we hung it up on their deer pole to drain, cool, and be seen. It was the first deer taken by the group that season, and I had shot him right at 7:00 a.m. I reminded them that I had shot the last deer of the season last year. That got some comments. My second deer season was done an hour after it started.

Since I already had my deer, I stayed at the farm and took my car apart to determine what I would need to fix it. The man that owned the farm took me to a junkyard where I bought the parts I needed, and then we went back to the farm and put my car back together. I hunted the rest of the afternoon as a dog without a gun to help the other hunters try to get their deer.

When we were done hunting for the day, my cousin and I told everyone goodbye, tied my buck across the back of my car, and headed for home. During the trip home, we saw several larger bucks tied across other hunter's cars, but I didn't see any I would have traded mine for. I'll never forget that hunt or that buck.

Our family ate good venison for a few months again, and I mounted the antlers on a plaque I made for them. I still have those antlers on my wall, along with many others that I have taken since then. But they will always be "my first buck."

It would be twelve years before I would do any hunting again.

Squirrel Tales to Game Trails And Shore Lunches

8   The Drought Years

That hunting season was the fall of 1966. I turned eighteen after the first of the year, and graduated from high school in June of 1967. The Vietnam War was still going on and it was just a matter of time before I would be drafted. In an effort to benefit from a bad situation, I enlisted in the Marine Corps for four years under a guarantee that I would end up in the air wing and get some related training in the meantime. At the time, that was as close as I was going to get to any further education. For the most part, it was a good decision.

I spent the next three years at various duty stations in the United States without any opportunities to hunt. The fourth year of my enlistment was spent in Vietnam. Following my discharge, I returned home to Michigan, high unemployment, and very limited job opportunities. After a year and two jobs, with one layoff, I needed a change.

Enter my dad again. At his suggestion I explored the

possibility of going to college, or at least getting some additional education, if I ever hoped to amount to much more than I was. I had my G.I. Bill benefits available to me, a desire to better myself, an idea of what I wanted to do, and as always, the complete support and encouragement of my mom and dad. With all that going for me, I knew I couldn't fail.

So I left home again, this time to go to college. I went to school full-time, worked several part-time jobs, and four years later I had a degree in engineering, a wife, and a job offer in Dallas, Texas. That was forty years ago, as of this writing. We changed jobs several times and raised a family. I also got back to hunting shortly after arriving in Texas. Currently, I live and hunt in Kentucky.

All total, I missed twelve years of hunting after that 1966 deer season. It was the fall of 1978 when I joined a deer lease in the Texas Hill Country, and experienced yet another method of deer hunting. The drought had ended and it was great to be hunting again. I spent the next fourteen years on the same lease in Lampasas, Texas. I ran that lease for the last ten years I hunted there, but more on that in the next chapter.

In case you are keeping score, I shot my first whitetail deer in November of 1965. I shot my biggest whitetail buck, body and antler, in November of 2015. That's 50 years between my first and my most recent deer, with a lot of them in between. And I'm not done yet. And in case you are wondering, I have no, none, nada trophies in any record books. Every animal I ever shot, including the does, was a trophy to me, or I would not have shot them. Every one of them provided many great meals for my family, too.

Squirrel Tales to Game Trails And Shore Lunches

9 Texas Deer Hunting

We were only in Texas two years when a friend of mine where I worked invited me to join a deer lease in the Texas Hill Country. I had hung my set of deer antlers on the wall in our office and that got us talking about deer hunting. We shared an office and an interest in hunting. He promised to let me know when there was an opening on the lease he was on.

When he finally told me there was an opening for another hunter on his lease and asked if I was still interested, of course I said yes. It had been twelve years since I had hunted deer, and I had never hunted on a place where you paid to hunt there. After he explained it to me, I agreed to go with him one weekend to look the place over and see if I still wanted to join his lease. I had to make my mind up fast, because deer season was only three months away, and if I didn't take the spot on the lease, someone else would.

In Texas, the majority of hunting all types of game is done on private property where the hunter leases the hunting rights from the land owner. They agree, either formally or informally, on a dollar figure, number of hunters, day(s), and season only or year around access, and usually renegotiate the terms each season for the following year. Texas also allows hunters to hunt from blinds and over feeders, so these issues are also usually part of any lease agreement. The price will vary based upon location, facilities, and quality of deer available, among other things. As a result of these variables, the price of deer leases can vary greatly, and can range from a few hundred dollars to many thousands of dollars per hunter. The cost usually becomes the limiting factor for most hunters.

For the hunter that cannot afford to lease a place to hunt, or just chooses not to, there is some public hunting available in the state. There are over a million acres of public land spread throughout Texas, and for a nominal fee is available for hunting. Based upon the overall size of Texas, a million acres is not a lot of land. What usually happens is that those areas that are readily accessible, or in close proximity to heavily populated areas, tend to be more heavily hunted, at least around the edges and during the first week or two of deer season. After that, hunting pressure drops off significantly. This situation is no different than hunting public land anywhere else. Remember my first experience with hunting on public land in Michigan? Thanks, but no thanks. I've been there, done that, and I've got the T-shirt.

The only real disadvantage to lease hunting is the additional cost. On the other hand, some of the advantages are that you have a specific place to hunt, and in most cases, you know who and where your fellow hunters are. You also usually have a pretty strict set of rules designed to prevent people from getting hurt. I happen to like these reasons, and as such, have been able to justify to myself spending a reasonable amount of money each year on deer leases.

That first lease consisted of one thousand acres of land with an old farmhouse on it that had electricity, hot water, toilet and shower, gas heater, kitchen, living room, and two bedrooms. There were five hunters allowed under the agreement, and the cost was a hundred and fifty dollars per hunter for one year. The property was easily accessible by pickup truck, unless it was raining, and then access was limited. Oh, and besides having a few horses and cows on the property, it had a lot of deer and turkeys on it.

Needless to say, after seeing the place for myself, I took the spot that was open. Then all I needed to do was figure out what I would need to hunt there. We held a preseason meeting where I met the other hunters and we discussed what each of us needed to bring for opening weekend. It was going to be great to hunt again. The planning and preparation, combined with the excitement and anticipation, was just as I remembered. It was almost more than I could stand.

I hunted that lease for the next fourteen years and saw a lot of things change during that time. That was the place where I shot my first, and most, of the turkeys I've taken, both in the spring and fall. That was where I shot most of the deer

I've taken over the years, too. And that was the place where I took my kids when they were little to see nature, wildlife, and the great outdoors at its best. I miss that.

By my fifth season on the lease, I was the senior man and responsible for all the lease negotiations, as well as enforcing the rules. Over the years, the annual lease rates went up almost every year, the size of the property actually decreased to approximately six hundred acres, and the number of hunters increased to ten. And to make matters worse, the last few years we hunted there the landowner had over two hundred goats on the place, along with sixty cows and a dozen horses. There was still deer and turkeys on the place, but not like there had been. Then the state reduced the allowable limit of deer that could be legally taken per hunter for that county from four to three. In other words, it just wasn't worth the cost anymore. We paid five hundred dollars per person the last year we hunted there.

During those fourteen years, I also had the pleasure, most of the time, of meeting and getting to know a number of different hunters. Some were a real joy to hunt with while others were told not to come back. Some took their hunting very seriously and others just liked to be there. Some brought their children along to share in the hunting experience and to learn to hunt. Some of those kids shot their first deer on that lease. I'll go into more detail about some of those hunters later on in chapter 17, where I touch on some of the various styles and tactics I've encountered, and compare them to mine.

It was hard to give that deer lease up, and we knew it would be difficult, if not impossible, to find another one like it. We tried but were unable to stay together the next season. Some found places to hunt while some of us didn't. I don't think any of the guys hunt together anymore for one reason or another. At least one of the guys has since passed away. That's a shame.

Texas Deer Hunting

I didn't hunt deer for the next two years while I searched for a place to hunt. It was at the coaxing of my daughter, Kyle Marie, that I got another lease. She said she wanted to learn to hunt and asked if I would teach her. Since she was "Daddy's Girl" that alone was reason enough to find another place to hunt.

I hunted on that lease for ten years, and Kyle Marie hunted with me for three of the early years, before she graduated from high school and went away to college. The first couple of years she preferred to just observe. She asked a lot of questions about hunting, and learned how to read animal reactions to things around them. She observed roadrunner parents teaching their young how to hunt. We watched a lot of beautiful sunrises and sunsets together. She learned why it's called hunting and not killing.

Kyle Marie also learned gun safety and how to shoot. She could shoot my .270 rifle as well as, or better than, I do, but wasn't yet ready to shoot a deer. She even passed up several nice deer, including a nine-point buck that I did shoot. After she helped me clean that deer, she told me she was ready to shoot one. The next season, she shot a nice six-point buck, and I was there to be a part of it. She did great. I'm very thankful that I had the opportunity to spend those quality times with her. That alone makes it all worthwhile to me. I mounted her buck's antlers and they are on the wall with mine. I'm more proud of those than I am of any of mine.

Kyle Marie had helped me process a lot of deer before she asked me to take her hunting. She was always a good helper. She now has a career, a family of her own, and lives in another state. Maybe I'll get a chance to teach her sons, my grandsons, to hunt, too. I certainly hope so.

Squirrel Tales to Game Trails And Shore Lunches

10   My First Elk Hunt

In 1989, I got the opportunity to hunt elk in Oregon. By then, I had already read everything I could find on elk hunting because I knew I would go someday. It was just a matter of time and it turned out to be everything I expected it to be.

In early 1988, a business associate and I were having a conversation over dinner one evening about hunting when we decided to seriously look at going elk hunting. I took this idea very seriously, and along with another business associate who was also interested in joining us, proceeded to put together an elk hunt for 1989. It had to be 1989 because we soon found out that it was already too late to obtain 1988 nonresident hunting licenses in most cases. This actually worked out very well as it allowed us time to do our homework and properly prepare for such a hunt.

We first explored the possibility of a do-it-yourself, unguided hunt on public land and quickly decided against it for various reasons. Due to the limited time we had, the expenses involved, the logistic requirements for tents, food, and vehicles, and not knowing the area, we felt it would be best to look into the price of a package hunt with the services of guides and an outfitter. This would at least ensure that we would be hunting where there were elk, and would also ensure a means of getting an elk out of the woods if we were fortunate enough to shoot one. My being very optimistic about getting an elk served to further emphasize the importance of that last point. In checking with various states, we also found several that strongly recommended we use a guide service or outfitter for the same reason, or we would have to demonstrate that we had a means of getting the meat out of the woods before we would be allowed to hunt.

As we began our search for an outfitter or guide service, we discovered very early on that there was a very wide range of services available, and that the price range for those services was even wider. Since none of us were independently wealthy, we were not able to do a high-priced hunt. However, since this could have turned out to be a once-in-a-lifetime hunt, we didn't want to buy into a hunt that didn't offer good prospects of at least seeing elk. After much research and effort, we settled on an outfitter in Oregon, and we contracted his services for the fall of 1989. By then, our group of hunters had grown to four. None of us had ever hunted elk before, so we had high expectations.

As the date of our hunt approached, we all coordinated our schedules to arrive in Portland, Oregon, the day before our hunt was to begin. We would then travel together to Pendleton, Oregon, where our outfitter would meet us at the airport. They would then transport us and all our gear to the hunting camp, where we would get a good night's sleep and begin our five day elk hunt the next morning. When the date finally arrived, everything went like clockwork. The drive from the Pendleton airport to camp was consumed with talk

My First Elk Hunt

of the events of the next five days. We were ready.

Camp consisted of several large military surplus tents with dirt floors and a wood stove in the middle of each floor. The accommodations were spartan, but proved to be quite adequate. Cots at least got our sleeping bags off the ground, but the dust from the dirt floors soon covered them anyway. Aside from the dust, it was great. The single light bulb that hung in the middle of the tent remained on as long as the portable generator was running. When it went out at night, it was time to go to bed. When it came on in the morning, it was time to get up. It was very basic, yet functional and practical.

A separate tent served as the cook tent, dining area, and social center. That was where we started and ended our days. We ate breakfast and supper there, and relaxed there in the evenings. It reminded me a lot of the community house in my earlier deer hunting days, and was a very comfortable place to relax, discuss the day's hunt, laugh, joke around, and share hunting experiences.

There was a small stable in the camp where the outfitter kept two mules for those times when he needed to go into a remote area in order to bring an elk out. It also had a couple of four-wheel drive ATVs, and their pickups were all four-wheel drive. They were quite capable of getting us, and our meat, in and out of the woods.

Rounding out the camp was a tent where they could heat water for a hot shower, a meat locker where we would hang our elk, and a two-seater outhouse where we could sit and think when the urge hit us. When it was cold out, you didn't think very long because the outhouse didn't have any heat in it, and it was quite drafty.

Upon our arrival in camp, we put our gear in our tent, met everyone else, and shot our rifles to make sure they were still sighted in correctly. Then it was time for supper, a little socializing, and finally off to bed to get a good night's sleep. I don't remember sleeping much that night, but I do remember one of the guys getting up in the night by request and adding firewood to the wood stove.

The next thing I remember was the generator being started and the light in our tent coming on. It was time to get up and get ready to go elk hunting. After brushing my teeth, stopping by the outhouse, and freshening up in a pan of warm water the cook had put out for us, I headed for the coffee pot in the cook tent. It was great to be alive. I didn't know what time it was, but it was still very dark out.

The cook had breakfast ready for us by the time the hunters and guides arrived, and we discussed the morning strategies for the hunt while we ate. We split up, two hunters per guide, and put our gear in our guide's truck. Soon the guides were ready to go and we left camp. It was still dark out, and would be for at least another hour, but we had a long way to go before daylight. I remember thinking that if my cousin had been there, he would be asleep in the truck before we were very far from camp. I miss him.

We were hunting 70,000 acres of private property that bordered a national forest on one side. The majority of the property was very rugged and steep, heavily wooded, and an ideal habitat for elk, black tail deer, and wild turkeys. During the next five days, we covered most of the 70,000 acres, and in doing so, discovered muscles we didn't know we had. We had no trouble sleeping the rest of the nights we were in camp.

It was just beginning to get light out when we stopped the truck on the two-track road we had been following. The plan called for me to get out there, walk straight into the woods until I got to the barbed wire fence, turn right, and follow the fence until I got to a creek. Once there, I was supposed to wait until the guide got there. We would then

My First Elk Hunt

decide what to do next. I was supposed to take my time and look for elk or elk sign as I went along.

The barbed wire fence separated the private property from the national forest. The federal property was open for hunting to the public and was therefore open to us to hunt on as well. That meant that people could be hunting on the other side of the fence and take advantage of elk crossing over the fence into the national forest. As I approached the barbed wire fence, there was, in fact, another hunter sitting on the other side of the fence. I wished him good luck and he did the same for me.

Having read extensively about elk hunting in preparation for this occasion, I had an idea of what to look for, or so I thought. Hopefully, I would recognize elk sign when I saw it. I really didn't know what to expect, but as I made my way to the fence and then on to the creek, I walked right into an area that just reeked and smelled gamey. As I looked the area over, I realized I was looking at an elk wallow that was being used on a regular basis. I skirted the area to keep from disturbing it, and continued on to the creek.

Between the elk wallow and the creek I crossed several trails that looked like cow paths. We had been told that cattle were pastured on this property during the summer, but had already been rounded up and taken off the property for the winter. Two of these trails crossed the barbed wire fence onto the national forest and led to the elk wallow I had found. The only cows using those two trails were cow elk, and probably the bulls, too. It looked like a great place to hunt.

The creek I was looking for was only a couple of hundred yards further ahead and ran through the bottom of a fairly steep and deep draw. After making my way to the creek, I found a spot to sit down and poured a cup of coffee from my thermos jug. Before I could even finish my coffee, the guide walked up and asked me if I had seen anything. It was only 6:30 a.m.

After I told him about the elk wallow and the trails that I had found, we agreed that I would find a place to hunt in that general area and I'd stay there until he came back later. He would go back to the area where he had left the other hunter and help him find a place to hunt. In any case, he would not be too far away, and if I shot, he would hear it and come to see if I needed any help. I told him I had a good idea where I wanted to sit. He told me to shoot straight, and that he would be back later, and then he walked back into the woods.

I went back up the slope about a hundred yards and sat down on a log at the base of a tree. I was able to see up and down the fence line in either direction approximately a hundred yards. I could see over the top of the hill to my left, the creek in the bottom of the draw to my right, and even part of the way up the other side. The two trails that crossed the fence were to my left and easily visible. I sat facing into the national forest with my back to the tree. It was 6:45 a.m.

I had not been there ten minutes when I heard what sounded like a cow walking through the woods. It was a slow, steady, plodding pace with sticks breaking and hooves hitting logs. I thought that there was at least one cow still on the property.

As I looked in the general direction of the noise, I saw a bull elk casually walking out of the timber on the national forest property. He was clearly on one of the trails I had looked at earlier, and would soon cross the fence into our property. If he stayed on the trail, he would go up the slope and right into the timber where the wallow was located. When he crossed the fence, he would be approximately fifty yards away from me. I couldn't believe it. There was a bull elk fifty yards away on the first morning of my first elk hunt,

My First Elk Hunt

and he didn't know I was there.

The outfitter had told us that we could legally shoot elk on the national forest property if we got the chance because it was open to public hunting. My best shot at the bull would, in fact, be while he was on the other side of the fence. Once he crossed the fence, he would be quickly out of sight in the timber. I decided to take my shot as he stepped into a small clearing just before he got to the fence.

I raised my rifle, took careful aim, and when he walked into the clearing, I fired. He stopped and stood there. I thought that I had surely missed somehow, but I remembered what the outfitter had told us the night before. He said that elk are tough animals, and as long as they are still standing, shoot them again. So I did. And he still stood there. By then, I was really beginning to wonder what was going on, so I shot again. This time the bull collapsed in his tracks. It was 7:00 a.m., and I needed to pee real bad.

I quickly went up to the fence where my bull elk lay on the other side. He was dead, so I put my rifle down and crossed the fence to get a good look at him. I was shaking all over and couldn't stand still. I had just shot my first bull elk, and it was a 5x5 (five points on each antler) at that. I couldn't wait for the guide to get there, or for my friends to see it, or to get it back to camp. What a morning I had already had, and now the work would begin.

I quickly tagged my bull, took a few pictures, and then crossed back over the fence to wait for my guide. I was anxious to see if he had heard me shoot, and if so, how long it would take him to get there. Within thirty minutes he came walking up and wanted to know if it was me who had shot earlier. I told him yes, and then pointed out my bull elk on the other side of the fence. He couldn't believe it, either.

After a round of congratulations and a few more pictures, we went to work field dressing my bull in preparation for taking it back to camp. Once it was field dressed, we dragged it under the fence and onto the private property. This was not easy to do with only two people, and was an indication of things yet to come.

We then walked back to the truck and drove to camp to recruit all the help we could muster up. Four of us returned with a truck and a winch with a thousand feet of cable. It took us the rest of the day to get that bull back to camp where we skinned it, quartered it out, and hung it in the meat locker. The main course for dinner that night was fresh elk steaks. Those were the best steaks I've ever eaten.

While skinning the bull out, we found that all three of my shots had hit him within a three-inch circle. The bull was as good as dead with the first shot. The third shot appeared to take out the bull's opposite shoulder, which explained why he finally collapsed. He was literally dead on his feet.

The guides and outfitter estimated the bull's age to be four and a half, and felt he was a mature breeding bull. One of the guides said a previous hunter in that area had reported seeing a good bull, and that they believed this was probably him. Everyone in camp was pleased for me, and all the hunters were hoping to do as well. The outfitter told us that I had beaten the odds for my first bull, and that it usually takes a hunter, on average, nine years of hunting before he gets his first bull. I've seen that statistic in an elk hunting article since then. I like to think I brought enough skill to the hunt to make it happen.

We celebrated my success that night after dinner with a round of drinks, and then we called it a day and went to bed. I was tired and would sleep great. Morning would come early for all of us. When we needed another log on the fire during the night, I got up and fed the fire. I did notice that it was cold in the tent, but I was more interested in getting back in my sleeping bag. We awoke to the sound of the

My First Elk Hunt

generator, followed by our light coming on, and four inches of new snow.

We hunted in the snow the next four days and it was great. I could say that now since I already had my bull and was only along to help in any way I could. I wasn't much help, as the rest of the hunters were unsuccessful. We had a great time and saw a few elk, but all proved to be cows and a small, spike horn bull. Too soon the hunt was over and it was time to return to civilization, reality, and schedules. We all agreed that we would need to do it again, as soon as possible, as we made our way home.

Like my first whitetail buck, there are certainly larger bulls out there, but I wouldn't trade mine for any of them. He's on my wall right next to that first buck, and surrounded by other bulls that are even larger. The big difference is, he will always be my first bull elk.

Squirrel Tales to Game Trails And Shore Lunches

11   My First Caribou Hunt

 Although my friends and I truly enjoyed our Oregon elk hunt, we decided that our next hunt should be for something with a much higher success rate than twenty-five percent.

With that, one of the guys suggested we hunt caribou in Alaska, because he had read that the success rate was one hundred percent. The idea had a lot of merit, and sounded like an exciting, once in a lifetime opportunity to all of us, so I started calling outfitters. I located an outfitter who specialized in Alaska barren ground caribou hunts, and after numerous phone calls and lots of questions, we finalized an Alaskan caribou hunt for the fall of 1990. The package included everything from one-on-one guided hunts and food and tent accommodations to round trip transportation, with Anchorage, Alaska, as our starting and ending point. All we needed to do was bring our warm hunting gear and rifles, and get to Anchorage and back. Nothing to it, right?

Right. Almost everything went just as planned. Please notice that I said "almost" everything went just as planned. We soon realized that everything is subject to change in Alaska, including the weather in October. The outfitter had warned us that, due to our hunting so late in the season (it was the last week of the season to be exact), that we should be prepared to spend a few extra days on the tundra in case the weather turned bad. Other than that, a broken tail wheel on one of the Super Cub airplanes delayed us a little, one guy had to leave early, one guy got caught on the tundra a few extra days, two of us left the tundra just ahead of the storm, and flight schedules didn't really mean anything. Oh, and then there was the bear that got into the meat cache and claimed it for his own. Who were we to argue with him? Other than those few issues, everything else went pretty well. It definitely helped that all of us were flexible with everything that came up.

Like before with our elk hunt, we all agreed to meet in Anchorage the day before we were scheduled to fly to the tundra where we would be hunting. We spent the night in a hotel in Anchorage and had dinner together. Needless to say, the excitement was running high as we tried to anticipate

My First Caribou Hunt

what the next week would bring. We were catching a charter flight early the next morning so we turned in early that night. Besides, it was cold out and we figured that we better enjoy the warm hotel accommodations while we could. We knew that we would be sleeping in sleeping bags in tents on the tundra for the next six or seven days, at least.

The next morning we took a cab from the hotel to the charter flight office, only to find that they were not open yet. As we stood outside in the cold and waited for someone to open the place, we watched the sun come up over the mountains. It had snowed during the night and everything was covered with a light dusting of new snow and frost. It was beautiful. It was great to be alive.

Eventually, a guy showed up who ran the charter operation, and he began to get two small airplanes ready for the flight from Anchorage to Illiamna. In the meantime, other people began arriving to catch the same flights we were waiting for. After another hour or so, we boarded the planes and departed Anchorage. One plane went directly to Illiamna, while the other made an intermediate stop to drop off passengers at another destination en route to Illiamna. Naturally, two of us were on each airplane, so we arrived at Illiamna at different times. It didn't really matter, though, because the Super Cub airplanes that were to take us out on the tundra were not there yet.

Illiamna, Alaska, I was told later, has a population of approximately five hundred people in the summer and only about one hundred who stay year around. The airport has a gravel runway with several buildings and a parking/storage area for small airplanes and the remains of small airplanes. The airport was closed when we arrived there, so we had to wait outside for our outfitter to get there. It was cold out, but we were really glad that it was at least dry and sunny. It was obvious that we were not going anywhere until someone showed up to take us there.

After about an hour of "cooling our jets," a small Super Cub airplane landed, taxied up in front of the buildings, and shut down. The pilot got out of the two-seat airplane, walked over to us, and introduced himself as our outfitter. He told us that he would take us into town, help us get our hunting licenses, and then, along with another Super Cub, shuttle our gear and us one at a time to the base camp on the tundra. By then we were ready to do anything other than stand around much longer. We all got in a vehicle the outfitter kept at the airport for the ride into Illiamna. It had no back window and the heater didn't work, but at least we were going someplace.

We went to a small general store where you could get the basics of just about anything, including our nonresident hunting licenses. By that time we were all hungry, so we grabbed some munchies to hold us over until we got to camp, then it was back to the airport for our flights out to base camp. A second Super Cub was waiting when we got back to the airport, so I put my gear in one of the planes and one of the other guys put his gear on the other airplane. Then we were off.

We would be hunting the barren-ground species of caribou found in Alaska, and specifically, the Mulchatna herd, which is estimated to number in the thousands. Like the name implies, they live on barren-ground tundra most of the year, subsisting almost entirely on lichen. Barren ground pretty well describes the area of the tundra we were hunting. Aside from the occasional willow bush patches where bears were known to hang out, a few beaver bogs that were not much more than low areas where water ran through and more willow bushes grew, the ground was fairly level, very barren, and almost totally frozen. It was almost completely covered in light green lichen that was only a half inch above the ground.

Picture hunting relatively flat ground that was virtually

My First Caribou Hunt

devoid of any plant growth except for the occasional willow bush patch or beaver bog for as far as you can see in any direction. To start with, the animals, caribou and bears, will probably see you before you see them. As long as you are a long way off, as in miles, they don't pay too much attention to you. When you get closer to less than a mile, they may become a little more interested in you. As you close the distance between you and them, they become quite alert and focused on you.

The barren-ground caribou are herd animals and make annual seasonal migrations. Depending upon the weather, availability of food, length of day, biting insects, and any other caribou migration triggers, you may encounter small groups of cows and yearlings migrating early in the season. Later on you may encounter large groups of cows, yearlings, and young bulls migrating through an area. Late in the season you will find the stragglers, including big bulls that are the last to migrate.

Since we were hunting the last week of the last hunting season, we did not expect to see large herds of caribou. We did fully expect to see small groups of late migrating harems of a dozen or more animals, each typically including a mature bull caribou.

All of these parameters boiled down to only one hunting method option: spot and stalk. And it was long distance spotting, long stalks, and more spotting to determine if the group included a good bull or not. If not, you did more spotting and more stalking. If it did include a good bull, you tried to put together a plan and stalk that would get you within a reasonable shooting range without spooking them.

Herd animals, including cattle, caribou, elk, and even elephants, are normally led by a matriarch or lead cow. This cow sets the tone and level of excitement for the herd. There may be a bull, or even several bulls, in the herd, but they are only there to attend to the cow's needs. As long as the lead cow doesn't get too excited, the rest of them don't either.

So add to the challenge of a stalk across barren ground with little to no cover of any sort the fact that "all eyes are upon you" from a long way off, and the need to identify the lead cow in hopes of not spooking her and causing her to flee and all the others to follow, and the hunt is on.

We abandoned one such effort on my hunt when we got close enough to see that the bull had one antler broken off. In another effort, my guide and I sat down on the tundra, probably half a mile from a group of caribou, and he waved a red handkerchief over his head. He told me to be still, but ready, in case a bull was in the area. Within thirty minutes, all the caribou in that group were within a hundred yards of us. There was no bull in the group, but I learned that curiosity in their nature could have filled a cow tag had we had one.

Base camp was sixty miles north of Illiamna and would take almost an hour to get to by a Super Cub. En route we flew over small bands of caribou that only served to further fuel our excitement. As we landed on the tundra near the base camp, I noticed a small wooden structure off by itself approximately two hundred yards from camp. When I asked what it was for, I was informed that it was where they kept the caribou meat, in case the bears decided to help themselves. It was better that they go there than into camp. It sounded like a great idea to me, especially when they told us they already had to kill one bear because he liked to raid the cook tent, and no matter what they tried to do to discourage him from doing so, he didn't get the message. I offered to move the meat cache an additional two hundred yards further from camp if they thought it would help. They thought I was kidding. I was not.

Base camp consisted of four wall tents and a three-sided,

My First Caribou Hunt

one-hole outhouse. The three sides offered limited privacy, served to break the wind, no pun intended, and provided incentive not to dally there very long. All three features were quite effective. All four of the tents had wooden floors and kerosene heaters. The cook tent was where all meals were served, while the other three tents provided sleeping arrangements for five people per tent. The wall tents proved to be quite warm and comfortable, especially when you consider the wooden floors, the cots, the heat, and a sleeping bag. And as for the meals, a camp cook prepared all the meals, including a hot breakfast and supper, and a cold lunch to go. Not bad at all for base camp, and if you were one of the hunters hunting from base camp.

However, only two of us would be staying in base camp. The other two would be flown further out on the tundra to spike camps, where we would hunt one-on-one with a guide. We would be dropped off one day, and picked up again five days later, weather permitting. Since no vehicles are allowed on the tundra, they fly hunters and their gear in and out, and hopefully their caribou back. While on the tundra hunting, you hike everywhere you go.

Alaska also requires that all nonresident hunters use a guide for several reasons. They want to make sure that nonresident hunters don't get lost on the tundra and end up bear bait, or costing a bunch of money to rescue them or recover their remains. They also want to ensure that the animal you shoot is removed from the tundra, meat as well as antlers. In fact, the rule requires that the meat be recovered prior to the antlers in order to reduce the chances of trophy hunters taking the antlers and cape and letting the rest of the animal go to waste. I agree with all of these rules.

Another rule they have is that you cannot hunt the same day you fly. This is intended to prevent hunters from spotting a bull from the air, landing near it, and shooting it. It has to do with "fair chase," and once again, I agree with it.

After dropping the other hunter and me and our gear off in base camp, the two Super Cubs returned to Illiamna to pick up our other two hunters and their gear. In the meantime, we were served a hot bowl of split pea soup and informed that when the planes returned, we would be flown out to spike camps, and told not to unpack any of our gear yet. That sounded good to me, so when one of the Super Cubs landed and dropped off another of our hunters, I was ready to go.

Once again, we loaded my gear and me, along with a week's worth of provisions for two, a bottle of whiskey, and a case of Coca-Cola in cans, into the Super Cub and took off. After about fifteen minutes of flying, we landed near a small canvas tent and an even smaller dome tent. I unloaded all my gear and the provisions, and the Super Cub took off for base camp. There was no one in camp, so I looked around, took a few pictures, and began to wonder what I was supposed to do next.

It was late afternoon and the shadows were long as the sun began to set. The day had been beautiful, bright, clear, and sunny. The sky was still cloud free and the temperature was well below freezing. Once the sun went down, it would get much colder. I was enjoying the raw natural beauty of Alaska at its finest when a guy walked into camp.

After a brief introduction, the guy explained that he was the hunter that had been in that spike camp all week, and that he had shot a bull earlier in the day about four miles from camp. The guide had been busy skinning and quartering the bull before he came back to camp for backpacks to carry the meat and antlers back to camp. Since I didn't have anything else to do, I offered to go with him and help pack his bull out. He accepted my offer, of course, and we headed back out to where his bull was.

When we got to the bull, the guide was ready for us. We loaded the two backpacks with meat, I took the antlers and

My First Caribou Hunt

cape, and we started off to camp. It was getting dark by then, and was very dark by the time we got back to the spike camp. We left the meat and antlers about two hundred yards away from camp, then went to the camp. It was too late to fix anything to eat, we were too tired to anyway, so we had a drink and went to bed. It was a cold and windy night, and I was glad I had had a bowl of split pea soup back at base camp many hours and miles earlier.

In the morning, we got up and had hot coffee while we waited for it to get light out. I was awake early so I chipped ice to make the coffee. We had a two-burner Coleman gas camp stove and a single Coleman gas lantern in the main tent, but no heat or wooden floor, let alone a cook to fix our meals. Between the camp stove and the lantern, it was not enough to even take the chill out of the tent. It was well below freezing, and never did get above eighteen degrees the entire time we were there. It was so cold in the tent that when the guide tried to make his cup of coffee in a plastic cup, the hot coffee caused the bottom of the cup to break and fall out. I was surprised he didn't know better than that.

The other hunter would be picked up during the day, while the guide and I would go back out to his bull to retrieve the remaining meat before the bears or wolverines found it. I was then legally able to hunt, so I carried my rifle in case we saw a good bull. We spent the rest of the day getting his meat back to camp and checking out several bands of caribou, looking for bulls. By the time we got back to camp the first time, the other hunter and all his gear had already been picked up. When we got back to camp that evening, the guide and I fixed a hot meal and had a drink or two. All the Cokes had frozen and the cans had swollen up. He was having a hard time trying to get a can to thaw out enough so he could drink it, so I showed him how I would do it. I used my hunting knife to cut the end off the can, and then dumped the frozen mass into one of those plastic cups. I then filled the cup up the rest of the way with whiskey and enjoyed a real good drink with my dinner. He thought that was pretty slick, so he had one or two himself. It was then time to get some sleep. It was another very cold night, but I slept great.

In the morning, I got up and got the Coleman lantern going, chipped enough ice to make coffee, and had it ready to serve when the guide got up. We decided that we would climb to the top of a high piece of ground about a mile away from camp and try to spot bands of caribou once it got light out. When we finished our coffee in metal cups, we headed for the high ground. We were anxious to get going so we could get warmed up. It was very cold and windy as we climbed the hill and tried to spot caribou. There was nowhere to get out of the wind, so we quickly got cold.

From our vantage point we were able to spot a Alaskan brown bear sow and her two cubs as they foraged for food. We agreed to stay away from them. We also spotted a band of at least a dozen or more caribou approximately six miles away, according to the guide. He was pretty confident that a band that large would have a bull with it, so I suggested we hike over to it and get a better look. Besides, I was getting really cold and was ready to take a hike just to warm up if nothing else. He agreed and we started off in their direction.

By the time we had hiked about halfway to the caribou, it was the middle of the day, so we stopped to have a lunch of frozen caribou meat, frozen cheese, and crackers. It was another beautiful, clear, crisp day, and as long as we kept moving, we stayed warm. When we stopped to glass the animals or to eat lunch, it got very cold, very fast. From where we were, we were able to see at least one bull, so we decided to continue on in order to get a better look.

When we got to within a mile of the caribou, I decided that I wanted to get a lot closer to the bull. He looked like a

My First Caribou Hunt

real good bull to me, and after the guide got a good look at him, he agreed. The stalk was on. In the next hour or so, we were able to use the available terrain to our advantage and closed the distance to less than one hundred yards.

We had managed to get a lot closer to the caribou than the guide thought we would be able to. The problem now was how to get a shot without spooking the cows. Every time I looked up, all I could see were cows. The bull had his head down grazing, surrounded by cows. All I could do was wait. Eventually, the cows dispersed enough that I was able to get a clear shot at the bull. At my shot, the bull went less than five yards away and dropped. The cows ran off a couple of hundred yards, and then stood there and watched us as we checked my bull. I peed, took pictures, and we congratulated each other on a great hunt. When we were finished cleaning, skinning, and quartering my bull, the cows were gone. I don't know where they went. We were both so busy processing the bull before it froze solid that neither of us noticed them leave the area.

We then had a decision to make. Do we hike back to our own spike camp where all our stuff was, or do we hike into base camp, which was about the same distance away? Tough decision, huh? We decided to hike to base camp where we could get a hot meal and sleep in a tent with heat in it. By the time we arrived in base camp, it was dark out. After another round of congratulations, a hot meal, and several drinks, we turned in on cots in heated wall tents. I slept like a baby.

The next day they sent a Super Cub out to the spike camp to bring my gear back to base camp. They also sent it out to where my bull was to bring in the meat and antlers. I didn't even have to pack my own bull out. Don't get me wrong, though, I'm not complaining. After all, remember that I helped pack another hunter's meat and antlers out earlier. I figure we're even.

Of the two hunters that had stayed in base camp and hunted out of there, one had taken his bull the day before and the other had already left to return home early, empty handed. The fourth hunter in our group was still out on the tundra hunting out of a spike camp. Three of us were done hunting, and the best we would be able to do would be a seventy-five percent success rate if he were successful.

While we were busy enjoying the beautiful morning, a game warden landed his plane and taxied up. He was making his rounds of various camps to check on hunter success and to inform those that were still in camps to get ready for a storm. He highly recommended that if we were done hunting, we should consider getting off the tundra and at least go in to Illiamna. The storm was predicted to hit that night and would probably last at least three days. It was up to us what to do. Another no-brainer, huh?

The two of us that already had our bulls decided to go back to Illiamna and stay in a lodge there rather than ride out three days of storms in tents on the tundra. It was a good decision. We spent that night in Illiamna and flew back to Anchorage the next day, just ahead of the storm. As for the fourth hunter in our group, he and his guide spent three days in one of the spike camp tents while the storm blew through. During that time, the storm also blew the other tent away, as in gone. Once the storm broke and the weather cleared, he and his guide literally stepped outside the tent and he shot his bull. When the Super Cub arrived to pick him up, he and his bull were ready and waiting.

The high temperature during our week on the tundra was eighteen degrees, and the low was a lot colder than that. When the high is only eighteen, the low doesn't seem to really matter. The spike camps had no heat, except for what a Coleman lantern and a two-burner Coleman cook stove gave off. I was pleasantly surprised at how much warmer a tent can feel with just a Coleman lantern going for light. I'm

My First Caribou Hunt

sure it was just my imagination.

As I mentioned earlier, all my days on the tundra were cold, clear, brisk, bright, and beautiful days. If we stopped hiking, we got cold. If we kept moving, we stayed warm. We simply kept moving as much as possible, even in camp. I truly enjoyed the entire experience. As for my fellow hunter who spent a few days in a spike camp tent during a violent storm, he has a few reservations about his trip, even though it was quite successful.

I described the outhouse arrangements in the base camp earlier. As for the restroom arrangements in the spike camps, we were on our own. Suffice it to say that they were considerably less accommodating then those in base camp. However, when I got to the spike camp, and the guide went to use the bushes, I asked him where the toilet was and he described a section of willow bushes a little ways away from camp and next to the water (ice) where we were camped. When he returned complaining about frostbite and the difficulties related to balancing while keeping your hunting clothes out of the way, I suggested that I'd make a camp toilet. He was all for it.

We had several white plastic five-gallon buckets. I used a bow saw to modify one of them by carefully cutting the bottom off it. You would then carry it to where you intended to do your business, put it down, and sit on it, and when you were done, picked it up and walked away. But even with that you didn't sit and think very long when it was that cold and windy out. It does solve the problem of balancing and keeping your clothes out of the works, though. I was amazed that the guide had not thought of it himself, but when I explained how it worked, he volunteered to be the first to test it. When he returned, he raved about it. He didn't appreciate the caribou cow that stared while he did his business, though.

Warm clothes, boots, and sleeping bags are necessities on a hunt like this, and can mean the difference between a great hunt and a miserable one. A wool blanket, insulated long underwear, and a good sleeping bag made sleeping possible. Even then, whenever I rolled over during the night, I found a cold spot and would instantly roll back over to the warm one.

All in all it was a tremendous hunting experience and adventure. Three of us succeeded in taking caribou bulls. For us mathematicians that's a seventy-five percent success rate. Only the guy who had to leave early didn't fill out, and he admits that he could have, but he just didn't see a bull that he thought he wanted before he had to leave. He is also the guy who suggested we hunt caribou in Alaska. Oh well.

In chapter 16, Always Learning Something, I describe how I have been able to observe and learn from animals in the wild. That's not to say that you cannot learn from fellow hunters, guides, landowners, Mother Nature, and "how to" resources. That's also not to say that you cannot teach fellow hunters, guides, and landowners a few things. As an example, my tundra port-a-pot I described earlier in this chapter. It will work anywhere you need it. I made one for a deer lease I hunted on in central Texas. Want to bet my caribou guide has used that trick ever since?

On a personal note, I have been blessed to hunt and fish in Alaska several times over the years and always look for a reason to go again. I took my wife and our two teenage children to Alaska for a week-long land tour, and a week-long cruise down the Inside Passage for our twentieth wedding anniversary. They all loved it and I was thrilled that I was able to share a memorable trip with them. We just celebrated our forty-first wedding anniversary and we still talk about that trip to Alaska, catching salmon, rafting the Kenai River, and flying the float plane to Tacu Glacier. It was worth every dime.

My First Caribou Hunt

Besides it being a great caribou hunt with good friends and succeeding in getting a very good caribou, I also learned a few things during my hunt that you may or may not know. I share them here because they were things that I didn't know until I went on this hunt.

You probably already know that Alaska is pretty big. They claim it to be twice the size of my beloved Texas. I have to believe them since I can't prove otherwise. But did you know that because of its size, terrain, and weather, many locations in Alaska are inaccessible by road? I'm not just talking about remote areas. Start with Juneau the state capital. How about Dillingham and Illiamna? There are many towns in Alaska that are landlocked and only accessible by air and/or boat. They may have roads and vehicles, but they all got there by boat or plane. Some small communities are linked by only train or air. Because of this a lot of Alaskans are private pilots.

A seasoned bush pilot told me that half the adult population of Alaska is licensed private pilots. He went on to say that only about half of them are current, which translates to "still legal to fly" and still familiar with the airplane they own/fly. This was in response to me mentioning that we had found the wreckage of a small plane on the tundra while hunting. He was not surprised at all. He told me there are a lot of small plane crashes in Alaska due to inexperienced private pilots exceeding their own or their planes limitations. Most lost their lives in the process. He told me that his flight instructor died in a crash on the side of Mount Illiamna, and his remains and the wreckage are still up there somewhere. Very little airplane wreckage is ever recovered due to unknown location or inaccessibility by vehicles.

This brings me to Mount Illiamna. On several flights on small airplanes out of and back to Anchorage, we flew through a long pass with high mountain peaks on both sides. Mount Illiamna is an active volcano north of Anchorage and on the east side of the pass I'm referring to. It is normal procedure for all small airplanes to radio ahead to the other end of the pass to get weather information in the pass before they commit to entering the pass. That is because the pass is too narrow to turn around in if you needed to. Small airplanes are not pressurized to fly above ten thousand feet. The mountaintops are higher than that. Any weather encountered in the pass would most likely prove to be fatal.

You would think that finding the wreckage of a small airplane on the tundra would be bad enough, but imagine my surprise when we found a large, as in probably three hundred foot-long, all-steel ship on its side on the tundra, six miles from the ocean according to my guide. That's right, a seagoing ship of freighter configuration. You can't make this stuff up.

Now, I know that the tides rise and fall as much as ten feet or more twice every day in parts of Alaska, but this is crazy. There's also an explanation in this case according to my guide. And supposedly, this isn't the only ship rusting away on the Alaska tundra.

It seems that the earthquake, and the tsunami caused by it, that hit Anchorage Alaska in 1964 not only did a lot of damage to the towns along the coast, it also deposited numerous ships and boats inland from the sea when the tsunami washed over the shore and land. Based upon the size of the ship or boat, and where it came to rest, some were recovered. Others were scavenged where possible, and the remaining ones that were too big to recover were left to deteriorate. The one I saw had already been there almost thirty years at that time, and will be there for a very long time to come.

So what do you do when you have a small, single engine floatplane frozen in the ice on a small lake on the tundra? It's illegal to leave it there until the spring thaw, so that's not

My First Caribou Hunt

an option. Floatplanes don't have tires, so you can't take off on the tundra even if you did get it out of the ice.

Duh. Why you fly it out of there, of course.

This is a true story. I was there. I was part of it. I couldn't believe it, but I saw it with my own eyes. Only in Alaska.

Now try to stay with me on this. I'll go slowly so you can appreciate what happened. What follows is a demonstration of Alaskan ingenuity, determination, creativity, and "can do" daring. And there was a lot of beer involved, too.

The day I was flown to base camp, I noticed a small lake not far from camp. On that lake was a small, single engine, high wing airplane. I don't remember if it was a Piper or a Cessna. At the time, I didn't give it a second thought.

After only a couple of hours in base camp, I was flown out to the spike camp where I hunted from for the next few days. Remember, the high temperature during our hunt was eighteen degrees. The ice was already forming on the lake and around the floats when we arrived.

Fast forward. We all hunted for several days. I shot my bull on the third or fourth day. Since my bull was down about midway between the spike camp and base camp, about six miles either way, my guide and I agreed that we could get a hot meal and a good night of sleep, in a heated tent, if we went to base camp instead of back to our spike camp. That was a no-brainer, so that's what we did. It was dark by the time we arrived in base camp. As we walked past the airplane on the lake, I noticed that the floats were heavily iced all around. I didn't give it another thought while I ate a hot meal, drank a hot cup of coffee, and got a good night of rest and relaxation on a cot in a heated tent. The two guys that had flown the airplane into base camp were still there when we arrived that night. They were also totally smashed and still drinking when I went to bed.

I got up early the next morning and went to the cook tent for a cup of hot coffee. I took my coffee and went outside to enjoy the bright, clear, beautiful, cold morning. A little later after a couple more cups of coffee, the two guys that the airplane belonged to got up and about. They were already drinking beer and discussing what to do about the airplane. It was obvious to me that they wanted to get it off the tundra before the big storm arrived. They devised a plan, presented it to us as if to get our approval, and then enlisted our help in implementing it. I thought about selling tickets to the main event, but there wasn't anyone around to sell them to.

Are you still with me? They have a plan. They toasted their plan and drank another beer. Then it was time to get busy.

Because it was so cold out, the first thing they needed to do was get the engine thawed out enough to start. They did this by hanging a lit catalytic heater up under the engine cowl and then wrapping the cowl in a sleeping bag to hold the heat in. They then went back to the tent to have a few beers and warm up. They went back to the airplane with axes and chopped the ice loose around the floats. They then went back to the tent to warm up and have a few more beers. They may have drank the beers before they warmed up, I don't really remember anymore. I wasn't counting, anyway.

Next, they took two 4x8 foot sheets of plywood off one of the wall tents, and with our assistance, took them down to the lake. With all our help, we were able to push the tail of the airplane down while they pulled and pushed the airplane up onto the ice. Once on the ice, we slid the airplane, tail first, to the edge of the lake. There we were able to push the tail down far enough for them to put one of the sheets of plywood under each float. Then we all went back to camp to warm up and have a beer or two. By this time, I was ready for some of that whiskey.

My First Caribou Hunt

When they decided it was time to go, they were both showing signs of intoxication. I was interested in what came next, or I would not have watched. We all headed down to the plane. They had a six-pack of beer for the flight. I don't know where they flew to, but I guessed Illiamna was their nearest destination.

This is where it got kind of sporty. One of the guys tied one end of a rope to the tail anchor point and tied the other end to a large rock on the bank of the lake. The rope was tight between the two attach points. Stay with me now. They then loaded their stuff on the airplane. I think they may have had another beer, too. Next, one of the guys told us what they were going to do, and what one of us needed to do and when. He then removed the sleeping bag from around the engine cowl and removed the catalytic heater. He threw all of that into the airplane. Then both of them climbed into the airplane and cranked the engine up. And it started. They sat there with the engine running for probably ten or fifteen minutes while the engine warmed up. Then it was show time.

The finale went something like this. The airplane was sitting on two sheets of plywood on the ice, solidly anchored by a rope to a big rock so that the airplane wouldn't slide on the ice. The men and their stuff are on board and the engine is running and warmed up.

Do you see where this is going?

Our only instructions were that when he gives us the signal, the pilot will rev the engine up to takeoff power, hold it there, and we will cut the rope. If everything went as planned, the airplane would slide across the ice on the sheets of plywood and lift off, leaving the plywood to slide to a stop on the ice and be returned to the wall tent.

He did, we did, and it did, just like they planned. In fact, I'm not so sure they hadn't done that before. I wonder if they had enough beer to get them to Illiamna. Don't you just love a happy ending?

And finally, from the "It's A Small World" category…

Remember when I told you that I was dropped off in the spike camp from where I would hunt? Remember how there wasn't anyone there when I arrived and that a guy walked into camp a couple of hours later? He was the hunter who had been in camp for a week, had shot a caribou just hours earlier, and was coming to pick up backpacks to carry the meat out? The meat and antlers that I helped carry out?

Anyway, think about this. My guide was telling me about this guy a couple of days later and mentioned that he was a hard client to please. He complained and whined about everything, and wouldn't lift a finger to help with anything, including fixing breakfast, lunch, or dinner, or clean up. He even had his own booze and never offered the guide a drink. To say the least, the guide didn't have anything nice to say about the guy. He was glad to see him gone.

The bull he shot was a nice bull, but nothing to write home about. In fact, the guide said he had passed up much larger bulls waiting for a Boone and Crocket class bull that never happened. He shot his bull in the "eleventh hour" of his hunt just to fill his tag. That's why they were so late getting it off the tundra and needed my help that day and the next.

My guide asked me right up front, early in the hunt, if I was planning on having my trophy mounted. I told him not unless it was a real monster. At the time, I only mounted antlers, and I always mount my own. Then he asked me if I would mind if he caped my bull out and used the cape. I told him it was his if he wanted it, and then I asked him why he wanted it. His answer surprised me.

It seems that his prior hunter was also a neck shooter and had ruined the cape on his bull, but still wanted it to be

My First Caribou Hunt

mounted. My guide showed me the cape and it was a real mess. My guide was trying to save this other hunter's hunt and trophy even after listening to him complain all week. I told him I prefer solid shoulder shots.

When I did shoot my bull, it had a long, beautiful white cape without any damage on it. My cape is on this guy's caribou trophy that he shot as a last resort. He probably doesn't even know it. By the way, he was a doctor from Dallas, Texas. I was still living in Dallas at the time. It really is a small world, isn't it? You're welcome.

Squirrel Tales to Game Trails And Shore Lunches

12   My First Moose Hunt

While we all had a great Alaskan caribou hunt, and three of us succeeded in getting bulls, we all agreed that we preferred to hunt together instead of separate like we did in Alaska. We also agreed to try something else, so when one of the guys suggested moose, it sounded good to the rest of us. With that decided, one of the other guys and I started looking for a moose hunt. We ultimately booked a guided hunt with an outfitter in Slave Lake, Alberta, Canada. When it came time to hunt, one of the guys was unable to make it at the last minute. The remaining three of us were able to schedule flights that arrived in Edmonton within an hour of each other, so the outfitter met us at the Edmonton airport. We proceeded from there to Slave Lake where we spent the night with the outfitter and his family.

The next morning we were up early and on our way to our moose camp where we would spend the next five days. After approximately a two-hour drive by pickup truck, we transferred our gear and ourselves to four-wheel drive ATVs for the eighteen-mile ride on logging roads to our campsite. It was quickly evident why we left the pickups where we did and why the ATVs were needed. It was September and the ground was not yet frozen. All the trails had been heavily traveled by logging equipment and large logging trucks and were deeply rutted, and in many cases, very muddy and full of water. Even the ATVs had a difficult time in some places. It was recommended that we wear our rain gear during the ride in, for good reason. We were all covered in mud by the time we reached camp.

We arrived midday on a beautiful Indian summer day, the temperature about seventy degrees. It was too warm to be hunting moose. We put our gear in our tents, had lunch, and relaxed until early afternoon. The guides and outfitter went about the business of putting the camp together while we helped in any way we could.

Camp consisted of a canvas tent for the hunters, another one for the guides and outfitter, and a third one for a cook tent, where the cook also stayed. Last, but not least, we had a "two-hole comfort station" nailed between two trees and located a short walk away. It didn't have walls for privacy, so before proceeding that way, we all agreed to announce our leaving camp, and to again announce our approach to the privy. It worked. Fortunately, the weather cooperated as far as that part of the hunt went.

In fact, the weather was too cooperative all the way around. We slept in the tents with the flaps open, and we slept on top of our sleeping bags. It might have gotten down to sixty degrees during the night, and up to the mid seventies during the day. We hunted in T-shirts all week, and never needed the tent heaters at night. The heat also caused the moose to lay up in the shade until after dark, and made them unresponsive to all our calling efforts. Through the course of the week, we saw one cow, and got a quick look at another one and the bull that was with her. One of the guys actually succeeded in taking a bull, the only one he saw.

There was one major impediment to our hunt that adversely affected our success. It was unfortunate, unmanageable, and beyond our control. It was a bunch of native hunters that were hunting moose in the same general area that we were. They had no consideration for our presence there, and even seemed to resent the fact that we were there. They went as far as to ride their four-wheel drive ATVs through our camp in the middle of the night once. Mind you, they were hunting at the time. Yes, hunting at night. It was perfectly legal for them to do, but not for us.

Native hunters are native Indians, and as such are exempt from the typical hunting and fishing rules and regulations we nonnative hunters are held to. Notice that I said nonnative, as in non-Indian. As nonresident hunters, we were held to an even stricter set of rules and regulations than the resident hunters played by. And, of course, that all translates into more limited and more expensive. But don't forget, we do similar things, including higher nonresident hunting license fees even between states, stricter limits, and even gender limits, let alone localized native hunter limits.

In Canada, and to some extent in the United States, the common term used to describe the differences in the rules, as they apply to native Indians and relative to the rest of us, is "subsistence" hunting and fishing. The native Indians were granted these lax rules and regulations as a result of treaties signed many years ago, allowing them to hunt and fish year around, as needed, to support themselves, both in food and in the sale of wild meat and fish to subsidize their income. Some will argue that they abuse the rules and regulations, but it is all legal in most cases.

It starts by anyone proving they are a certain percentage, by ancestry, of native Indian, and in most cases requires them to be a member of a recognized Indian tribe. There may be other minimal requirements or rules, but they vary from area to area, state to state, and may or may not be enforced.

As an example, I was salmon fishing in Canada a number of years ago, and as a nonnative, nonresident, I paid the highest price for my fishing license. It allowed me to fish for three days and only keep three fish. The fishing was good and the salmon was excellent eating, but it was the most expensive meal of salmon I've ever eaten anywhere.

I was only allowed to use conventional tackle, and was required to hire a local guide to ensure, under the guise of my own safety, that I didn't get lost, drown, or catch too many fish. Right. I think it was a conspiracy to support the local economy by putting local fishermen to work. Fortunately, I had my own tackle.

In the meantime, there was a lot of conversation and complaining by my guide about the native fishermen and how they could do anything under the auspices of subsistence fishing. It started with their fishing licenses, which are free for them. They can run gill nets across rivers to net salmon swimming up steam to spawn, a practice illegal to everyone else. They are supposed to check their nets daily, but don't normally do so. When they do catch a lot of salmon, they are allowed to sell it as part of their "subsistence," another practice illegal to everyone else. Subsistence obviously means more than just enough to feed their family a regular meal of salmon.

The worst abuse I observed on that same fishing trip was a small fishing boat loaded down with net-caught salmon tied up at a dock. You could smell the spoiled, rotting fish a hundred yards away. It was disgusting. Everyone in the area was quite upset and vocal about how this particular native fisherman had done this before. For whatever reason, every one of those fish went to waste. It was clearly an abuse of

My First Moose Hunt   103

native subsistence fishing rules. And they were worried about me keeping more than three salmon?

But now back to our moose hunt and our experience with what I refer to as no-holds-barred, anything goes native subsistence hunting. Yeah. Anything goes with these guys, and did while we were there among them.

Like I mentioned earlier, our hunt was during an unusually warm Indian summer with daytime temperatures in the seventies. It was beautiful weather, but just not conducive to good moose hunting. It was too warm for the moose, too. They were all bedded down in the shade all day, and only moved if they were pushed out of bed by hunters getting too close to them. Beyond that, their normal activity seemed to be restricted to the hours of darkness.

Of course, we moose hunters were restricted from hunting after dark and before daylight. How inconvenient for us, huh? But that wasn't so for the native subsistence hunters. They could hunt 24-7. Yes, even at night with spotlights. We hunted hard during the day while the moose and native subsistence hunters slept in the shade and rested up for their late night activity. Once it got dark, we tried to sleep while the moose and native subsistence hunters tried to do their business.

These guys can legally hunt at night, off powered vehicles such as ATVs using flashlights to "spotlight" the moose, and can kill any gender and number of moose. It's true. It's also sickening when you see the abuse and waste.

One morning my guide and I came upon five or six of these guys along a two-track trail we were traveling down while hunting. Naturally, we stopped to see what all the excitement was about. One of them had killed a small bull moose during the night and had radioed his buddies for help with cleaning it and getting the meat back to their camp. I couldn't help but notice the general party atmosphere and excitement level among them. As a fellow hunter, I could certainly relate to that feeling of success and accomplishment. However, those feelings were short lived when I observed what they were doing and how they did it.

There was three four-wheel drive ATVs on the scene. One of them had a two-wheel trailer behind it. In looking at the rifles bungee-corded to the ATVs, I noticed that several of them were old military surplus .303 British Enfield's. All had the wood still covering the barrel, the bayonet lugs were still there, and the tip-up rear peep sights were fully functional. In other words, there was not a scope on any of them. Just the military open sights. Oh, and by the way, there was a flashlight taped to the forearm of each rifle, and a piece of white rag tied on the end of the barrel at the front sight. This arrangement was clearly intended for point-and-shoot spotlight hunting at night. This was all legal for them.

As we stood there and talked with these guys, and observed their progress, it was clear that all of them were well versed on what was happening. In a matter of less than thirty minutes, they removed both hindquarters without skinning them, and put them in the trailer. They then removed the hide from along the back straps, and removed the majority of the back straps. I say majority because they never actually moved the carcass. They also didn't open it up or attempt to recover any other meat from the carcass. In other words, every bit of the moose was left to go to waste except for both hindquarters and some of the back straps. They didn't even take the front shoulders. All of this was very wasteful, but legal for them. And then they all drove away. I couldn't believe what I had observed. It's easy to see why so many other hunters are disgusted with subsistence hunting abuses.

Their rifles were of particular interest to me because I, too, happened to be hunting with a military surplus .303 British Enfield. Mine, however, did not look at all like theirs, and unless you knew what to look for, you wouldn't recognize

My First Moose Hunt

it as such. I had fully customized mine many years ago with major modifications to the wood and barrel, and the addition of sporting sights and a variable power rifle scope. When I mentioned the fact that I was also hunting with a .303 British, one of the guys looked my rifle over carefully, complimented me on how nice it looked, and told me he preferred his to mine. Of course he would. The scope was not any help when it came to spotlighting moose. Silly me.

On a separate note, and in all fairness, I have to tell you that I met a deer hunter in Kentucky a few years ago that hunted with rifles and archery. Okay. He also told me that he brought his deer back to his home intact. In other words, he did not field dress his deer. In fact, he didn't gut them at all. He told me that he hung his deer by its neck, split the hide up the back to the base of the neck, and then removed the hide from both hindquarters and fully exposed both back straps. He carefully removed both hindquarters and both back straps. That's all the meat he removed from a deer. The rest was wasted when he disposed of the carcass. He said it wasn't worth the trouble or the time to remove any remaining meat. What a waste, and probably illegal, too.

I didn't ask him if he was a Native American. I do wonder how many other so-called hunters do the same thing. I totally disagree with this action and waste of an animal. There's a lot of good venison in the tenderloins, front shoulders, neck and trimmings, and the heart, and if you know someone who likes liver...

As for our moose hunt, don't get me wrong. We were disappointed that we hadn't seen any more moose than we did, and certainly that we didn't have better luck than we did. But as far as the people, the weather, the food, and the efforts on the part of the guides and outfitter, it was a good hunt. We can't always be successful, and that's why it's called hunting and not killing.

The northern lights danced for us almost every night, and even during a couple of mornings when we first got up and about. We found bear sign in a creek bed one afternoon, and the outfitter believed it to be an adolescent grizzly bear. According to him, it was too big to be a black bear, although there were a few of them in the area also. And one night, while we sat around our campfire, we heard wolves howling in the distance. I had never heard wolves crying in the wild before that, nor have I since. I often wonder if any of my children or their children ever will. For that matter, will I ever again?

And then it was time to return to reality again. We packed up our gear, put on our rain gear, and rode the ATVs back the eighteen miles to where we left the pickup trucks. We returned to Slave Lake and spent another night there with our outfitter and his family in their home. Dinner was especially enjoyable, and we were just part of the family for a little while.

The next morning we were up early to say goodbye to everyone, and then we were off to Edmonton to catch our flights home. All too soon another hunt had come and gone, except in our pictures and in our memories. I have hopes of doing another moose hunt another day, the Good Lord willing of course.

Squirrel Tales to Game Trails And Shore Lunches

13 My First Mule Deer Hunt

My first mule deer hunt was the result of a combination elk and mule deer hunt that we did a few years ago with an outfitter in northwest Colorado. We had hunted elk with this outfitter the year before during their last hunt of the season. It was while we were hunting elk that we saw a lot of mule deer, especially when we were hunting the higher elevations. After further discussions with the outfitter, we booked a combination hunt with him for the following year.

It was a standard five-day hunt with the intent of hunting elk our first priority. The mule deer would be incidental to the elk hunt, or hunted exclusively after our elk had been taken. As it turned out, I was fortunate enough to take my bull elk the first day, and had the next four days to hunt for a buck mule deer. This worked out well, because where I shot my bull elk and where we hunted mule deer was approximately sixty miles apart. By having already taken my elk, I was able to concentrate exclusively on taking a good mule deer buck.

The area we hunted was very rugged and contained large draws with heavy sagebrush cover. We would drive into the area and stop on a high point where we could glass the surrounding draws and ridges with spotting scopes and binoculars. Once we spotted deer, we would attempt to get close enough to determine if there were any good bucks in the bunch. This type of hunting reminded me a lot of my caribou hunt in Alaska in that we did spotting first, then a stalk, and due to the time of the year, you could expect to find the bucks with the does.

The outfitter informed us that we were a little early for the rut, but that they were starting to see more and more mule deer bucks every day. All we could do was "look hard and go high" if we hoped to get a shot at a decent buck. The other thing was that all the young bucks were the first to start chasing the does, so we could expect to see a lot of them, too, and we did.

It was a lot of fun to just watch the deer. The does were very active, and the bucks were not far behind them. It was hilarious to watch a doe trying to go about her business while four or five young bucks followed her everywhere she went. Occasionally, we would get a look at a pretty fair buck, but he usually didn't hang around long enough for us to get too close. The bigger and older bucks were still up high and would not come down until the rut was in full swing, or until the snow got too deep up high.

On the second day of hunting for a mule deer buck, we spotted one that looked pretty good, so we made a planned approach and stalk on him. I hoped to get close enough to get a good look at the buck without spooking the does he was with. After driving as close as we dared, we walked and crawled to where we thought the deer were in the sagebrush.

The deer were on the opposite side of a draw, if we were correct, so I set up in a spot where I could see that side of

My First Mule Deer Hunt

the draw. The guide then went another hundred yards or so further up the ridge to try to get the deer to move up the draw toward me. Before he got to where he wanted to be, the deer began to move. They were not spooked or running, but they were moving up the draw as planned. I was surprised at how many deer were in the draw. Then I saw a nice, tall, classic 4x4 mule deer buck moving through the sagebrush, so I waited for a clear shot and took it.

At the shot, he bolted and ran about twenty yards before collapsing dead. The rest of the deer continued out of the draw, including another much larger buck that went up and over the top of the next ridge. Oh well. I didn't know there was another buck with the bunch until then, and neither did my guide.

But once again, I had a nice mule deer buck, and I'm not disappointed, even today. He was the first, always will be, and is currently a proud part of my collection of antlers. It was a great time and a great hunt.

Just to let you know, mule deer meat can be quite gamey, especially during the rut and when they are feeding on a lot of sagebrush. My plan all along was not to get too fancy with the processing of my trophy. I kept it real simple. One hundred percent of my mule deer went through a meat grinder, twice, in the process of becoming sausage. It was excellent.

Squirrel Tales to Game Trails And Shore Lunches

14 More Elk Hunts

Much like chapter 9 where I generally described my later years of deer hunting in Texas, I felt it necessary to also include a chapter where I generally describe my later years of elk hunting. Like the terrain where we hunt elk, the hunts themselves have high points and low points. Our tendency to remember the high points sometimes clouds our memories of the low points. Some of my most cherished memories do not include shooting something, but instead are of a specific place, a particular sunrise or sunset, or a friend I hunted with. Even my worst day afield was where I wanted to be.

I have been fortunate to hunt elk as often as I have, and I recognize that many hunters never get the opportunity to for whatever reasons. Like I said earlier, even a do-it-yourself elk hunt can be quite expensive, and the price only goes up from there. For that very reason, I strongly recommend that anyone seriously considering an elk hunt carefully evaluate all the costs involved in do-it-yourself hunts, and then shop around and compare it with a guided hunt. In my opinion, the additional expense for a guided hunt is justified, within reason of course, in the quality of the experience and the increased chances of being successful. There is never a guarantee when it comes to hunting, but there are some things that do improve your chances. Reputable guides are near the top of that list. Good guides can save you a lot of time, money, and work.

I have heard it said from two separate sources that the average do-it-yourself elk hunter will, on average, hunt nine to thirteen years before they kill their first elk. All that means is that you could get really lucky and kill an elk on your first elk hunt, or you could be really unlucky and not kill one in over twenty years of trying. Each hunt costs money.

In either case, guided or do-it-yourself, do your homework before you go, and be prepared for possible weather conditions, access, unexpected expenses, retrieving the meat, processing it, accommodations, time constraints, etc. This information is available online and from local resources where you plan to hunt for the do-it-yourself hunters. On the other hand, if you decide to use a reputable guide or

More Elk Hunts

outfitter, they will provide you with a thorough list of what you need to do and bring with you. They will also clearly tell you what they will do and what they will not provide.

Carefully consider what you get before you hire a guide or outfitter. These assisted hunts come in a large variety of sizes, shapes, and prices. On the spartan end of the spectrum you could find outfitters that only provide drop camp services. All they do is transport you, your gear, and your friends into the woods, mountains, etc., and drop you there. They then leave you to your own devices, with the only additional contact being that they will transport you, your gear, your friends, and your elk, if you killed one, back to civilization in however many days you agreed to. You do the rest. It's not much more than a do-it-yourself hunt.

At the other end of the spectrum are outfitted and guided hunts where you, your hunting clothes, and your rifle are all you bring with you to the hunt, along with payment in full. They provide everything else, such as a lodge, warm and dry beds, indoor plumbing, heat and lights, a camp cook, a personal guide, all necessary means of transporting you to the field, getting your trophy cleaned, and getting you and your trophy retrieved from the field, even delivering your trophy to a local packing house.

They do not pay for meat processing or shipment of the meat to a location of your choice. You have to take care of that yourself. The same goes for your trophy if you decide to have a taxidermist mount it for you. They may recommend a local taxidermist if you don't have one at home. If you decide to take it to a taxidermist at home, you'll need to make and pay for all arrangements to make that happen. These are only some of the costs you can encounter after your hunt, and they can add up fast. These costs would apply to a successful do-it-yourself hunt, too.

And then there are a lot of options in between spartan

and the package hunts. Do not be bashful. Ask questions. Ask for references and then call them. Ask about special accommodations if you or a fellow hunter has any dietary or physical limitations. Ask for a detailed list of all basic and customary expenses and charges. This will include suggested tips for your guide, your camp cook, and your outfitter. They will be quick to tell you what they do not provide.

Make sure they can provide whatever means necessary to get your meat and trophy out of the woods and back to camp. That may include vehicles, such as pickup trucks, ATVs, and even larger trucks with winches and long cables. It could mean packhorses or mules. It could mean even quartering the animal out and packing all the pieces in backpacks, preferably theirs, not yours. I've done every one of these at least once. Ask what services they provide in their package. Some may charge extra for these services, or contract them out to someone else for a fee.

Elk tend to hang out in timber and steep, rugged country. This alone will test your determination and physical ability. I was hunting elk with one of my friends in Colorado a few years ago when we slipped in on a bull in some of the worst terrain I've ever been in. After we busted our butts getting in there, and on him, we asked ourselves if we really wanted this bull bad enough to shoot it where it was. Since I was the shooter, he left the decision up to me. I asked him if we could get it out of there and he said we would, one way or another. It would have required packing the pieces out and probably taken a couple days to do. Due to all the factors involved, including that it was late in the day, I declined and told him I'd wait to catch the bull out in the open at a later date. My friend told me he was really glad I decided not to shoot, and then he said something about seeing his son graduate from high school.

I have since hunted deer in similar terrain in Kentucky. I

More Elk Hunts

never had any trouble getting in there because there were a lot of trees to break my fall. Those same trees kept me from falling back in when I tried to climb out again. It was so steep and rugged that I was glad I did not shoot any deer there. How steep was it you ask? I told the landowner that I believed I would have had to cook and eat any deer right where it lay in there, because I didn't think there was any other way of getting it out. He just laughed. I was serious.

One of our hunts included riding horses to the areas we hunted each day. The accommodations were great, the weather cooperated, the horses behaved themselves, and the scenery was absolutely breathtaking. Out of about ten hunters, only one got a shot at a bull elk, and it was on the last afternoon of the hunt, less than a quarter mile from camp. I did see one cow elk during the week, and it, too, was on the last day of the hunt, and was only two hundred yards from camp.

The program went like this: up at 4:00 a.m., breakfast by 5:00 a.m., and a ride up into the mountains in the dark. The goal was to be where we would be hunting before daylight. We did this every day of the hunt. We would hunt until lunchtime when we would enjoy a bag lunch while we rested our backsides and the horses. After a relaxing time, we mounted up and proceeded to where we would hunt for the afternoon. We would hunt our way back down the mountain and back to camp with the idea of being there before it got too dark. After the first day, we turned our horses loose and they returned to camp without us. We slowly walked back to camp, hunting as we went. At least it was downhill all the way.

Now I've ridden horses more than a few times in my life, so I knew we were climbing some very steep trails when we left camp the first morning. After daylight, it was clear that we had climbed quite high as well. I was thankful that we had horses to ride instead of having to make the climb on foot.

From where we were hunting you could see forever. Most of the mountains were still covered in green, but the aspens had already lost their leaves. With the first light, the sky, clouds, and slopes were a continuous changing tapestry of color. It was awesome and inspiring to watch. Man is not capable of creating such beauty.

Since it was our first day of hunting, we rode the horses back to camp that evening. It was still light out when we started down, and as we proceeded, I soon realized just how steep and narrow the trails were. The horses went single file, picking their way along the steep, rocky, and very narrow paths with us on their backs. To further complicate their steep descent, they had to navigate around trees and brush while stepping over logs, rocks, and other obstacles. The path, or trail, could not have been over a foot wide.

On one side it was very steep uphill, and on the other side it was very steep downhill. If the horse slipped, it would be a mess as the horse and rider went over the edge, so to speak. Sure, the trees would eventually break your fall, but with everything else that would be broken by then, who would care? It would not be a pretty sight.

It was during our ride down the mountain that I experienced another breathtaking view. It was also at that point that I figured out why we climbed these hills in the dark. No one in his right mind would do it in the daylight. As it turned out, we only had one horse slip once, and he didn't go over the edge. The horses were much more sure-footed than we wanted to believe, and their night vision was definitely better than ours. As for me, I was thankful my night vision wasn't any better than it is.

From that day on, I made a point of being very nice to my horse. I went as far as to make sure he had an apple everyday at lunchtime. One of the guides saw me give my horse an apple one day and joked that I was spoiling him. I assured the guide that that was my intention. Hey, whatever it takes, huh? It worked for me, and was a small price to pay as far as I was concerned. I did notice a few other hunters giving their horses apples at lunchtime, too, after that.

We have hunted several times with an outfitter in northwest Colorado, and have always had a great time. The hunting was excellent, the accommodations were great, and the people were fabulous. From the first time we met them, we were treated like part of their family. They went out of their way to ensure that our hunts exceeded our expectations. They worked very hard to put us on multipoint bulls, and stopped just short of guaranteeing us a bull. The only reason they wouldn't do that was because the decision to shoot, and the actual shot, was up to us.

These people have a true love and respect for the elk, as well as a thorough knowledge of them. These people explained early on that there are only two kinds of bull elk: good bulls and great bulls. All the bulls are good bulls. The only difference is that a great bull is one where you can drive a pickup truck in to, to bring it out. I totally agree.

The Good Lord willing, I hope to hunt these magnificent animals a few more times before I'm through hunting. If at all possible, it'll be with these same fine folks I'm proud to call my friends. God bless you all.

Squirrel Tales to Game Trails And Shore Lunches

15 Respect For Our Game Animals, Alive and Dead

I have a strong belief that, as hunters, we should have and demonstrate a great deal of respect for all animals, especially the ones we hunt. That belief has formed the basic underlying theme of this book, and I hope it sets the foundation for all hunter ethics and our sport. I touched on the subject early on when I mentioned knowing my limits and the limits of my guns. I brought it up again when I stated that I don't shoot anything that I'm not going to use. And finally, I mentioned respect at the end of the last chapter in reference to an outfitter I know.

Please don't misunderstand me. I have shot my share of "innocent" birds, turtles, and other animals over the years. It's just that I realized a long time ago that paper targets

120   Respect For Our Game Animals, Alive and Dead

often present more of a challenge and are easier to come by. They also don't go to waste or die a slow lingering death if you only wound them.

When it comes to the actual hunt, hunters have certain advantages over the animals we are hunting. Whereas they are generally creatures of habit caught up in a daily battle for survival, we are able to exploit those habits, analyze them and even apply deductive reasoning, and gain an advantage wherever possible. Where nature has endowed them with heightened senses, we have developed, and apply, means to counter those senses. In our quest for a successful hunt, we all too often are tempted to cheat in order to get the upper hand. Since we already have the advantage, is it really necessary to cheat? Is it really sporting? I guess it would be different if they were able to shoot back instead of just elude us.

As for the actual act of killing, be it by whatever legal means, I believe we owe it to the animal to be as proficient and efficient as possible. This goes back to knowing one's own limitations, as well as the limits of your weapon. If you've done much hunting at all, I'm sure you have taken at least one shot that was "iffy" at best, only to wound an animal and have it get away. I know of two such cases in my own experience where I still wish I hadn't shot. In one case, I'm positive the buck later died, and in the other, I'm confident the bull elk survived.

I once hunted with an outfitter who swore the only bad shot was the one you didn't take. Think about that. Please notice that I said I hunted with this outfitter once, and only once. I strongly disagree with that opinion. That attitude applies in basketball, not in hunting. That attitude, when combined with a hunter who is not proficient with his weapon, can only lead to wounded or crippled animals that may or may not survive. Those results only reflect badly on the rest of us. Once you've pulled the trigger, it's impossible to get the

Respect For Our Game Animals, Alive and Dead

bullet back. Once you've let the arrow fly, it's impossible to get it back. If we make sure we have a good shot to start with, we have a much better chance of making the shot, and a better chance of being successful. Wait for a good shot. We owe it to the animals and ourselves.

Always give careful consideration to your weapon of choice, be it rifle, archery, or muzzleloader, and your proficiency with it. Ensure that your choice is more than adequate for use on the game animal you are hunting. Always use enough weapon to make a good clean kill when you place the shot correctly. It's better to have more than enough, than not enough.

Case in point: I have taken a caribou and several elk with a .270 Win. Mag. I have also taken several elk with a .338 Win. Mag. The caribou and elk shot with the 150 grain, .270 Win. Mag. all stopped the bullet. One of the elk I shot with a 225 grain .338 Win. Mag. also stopped the bullet. Elk are tough animals. Like the outfitter told me on my first elk hunt with the .270 Win. Mag., "When you shoot the elk, keep shooting until it goes down. They can carry a lot of lead a long way." I believe him. All of those shots were good, well-placed shots. The fact that elk can absorb the energy and shock of those bullets confirms what the guy said.

This is even more important if you chose to archery hunt. Even with the modern archery equipment we have available today, the chances of wounding an animal increases exponentially. It's simply because of the nature of the weapon and the need for the hunter to know his and his equipment's limitations, and for him to be very proficient with the weapon and never exceed those limitations.

Simply put, an arrow must be shot into a vital organ, in most cases, in order to ensure a clean and quick kill. Even then, you will probably wait at least thirty minutes or more for the animal to bleed to death before you pursue it. An arrow rarely drops an animal in its tracks, unless the arrow breaks the animal's back, and that doesn't always happen. When it does, it usually requires another killing shot to finish the animal off humanely.

As a comparison, a rifle bullet travels at more than 2,000 feet per second in most cases. A fast arrow travels at 350 feet per second. Deer "jump the string" because sound travels faster than the arrow, so they hear the arrow release and react. This reaction can cause a shot to hit the animal in an area other than where you were aiming, and may lead to a wounded animal escaping. Bullets, because they travel faster than the speed of sound, allow for longer shots, and eliminate the chance of the animal hearing the shot before it hits it.

Gravity pulls bullets to earth just like it pulls arrows to earth. It just pulls arrows to earth faster because they are moving so much slower. This can cause a bad shot on an animal that is too far away from the hunter, and might result in a wounded animal. If you are lucky, you'll miss the animal completely. The same holds true for the bullet, but it happens at a much greater distance.

Bullets retain more energy downrange because they start out with more energy and speed. Arrows don't start out with a lot of energy or speed, and lose energy and altitude quickly because they are very slow. This can also result in a bad shot, or if you're lucky, a miss.

Case in point: I was processing a Texas buck quite a few years ago, and when I was skinning it out, I found a large cartilage mass along the spine. It did not appear to be a growth or tumor, and it certainly didn't appear to have affected the deer's movement in any way. It was about the size of a baseball and white. I carefully removed it and satisfied myself that the meat was okay for consumption. I carefully cut into the mass to try to identify it. What I found

Respect For Our Game Animals, Alive and Dead

was a three-bladed arrowhead completely encased in the cartilage. Think about that and what the deer went through, and it still survived.

In another case in Kentucky while I was cleaning a doe, I found not one, but three pieces of an aluminum arrow shaft in her shoulder and ribs. The three separate pieces totaled almost six inches.

In both cases, the shots were not fatal. In both cases, a rifle bullet in the same places would have killed the animals with little or no suffering.

Having said that, I have also killed a couple of wounded deer over the years. One was a small five-point buck that had its right front leg hanging by a piece of hide when I saw him. It had been shot several days earlier and would have been easy prey for coyotes. The right front shoulder was full of infection and stunk. Would he have survived had I not shot him? I doubt it. How long would he have suffered before dying? In this case, good shot placement with a rifle was lacking for some reason.

As for muzzleloaders, they fall somewhere in between rifles and archery, and require careful consideration when using them, too.

Always ask yourself these questions: Just because the weapon can be used for the hunt, is it the best choice? Are you proficient with it, and if not, should you consider another choice? You owe it to yourself and the animal you are hunting.

Once the animal is dead and properly tagged, and the pictures have been taken, promptly clean it and process it to prevent waste. Most wild game tastes strong and gamey, or in worse cases, is ruined and goes to waste because the hunter fails to properly field dress the animal or properly cool the carcass quickly enough. Not knowing any better is not an acceptable excuse. Knowing what to do after the shot is as important as knowing what to do before the shot. With the shot, the hunt is over and the work begins. Even if you do not intend to use the meat yourself, at least process it so that someone else can use it and it doesn't go to waste. Trophy heads are nice, but meals of wild game are excellent if the animal is properly processed and handled immediately after the animal is dead.

I assure you, if we were to treat prime beef the way some people treat wild game, the beef would taste bad, too. An important part of every hunt must include the recovery of the meat, as well as the trophy head. That's why some states like Alaska and countries like Canada require nonresident hunters to show means of recovering the meat before the head or antlers are recovered. I think this is a great idea, and it should apply to all hunters, no matter where we hunt.

I, like most hunters, take a great deal of pride in my successes and am proud to show off my trophies. However, in today's society, not all people necessarily agree with our actions, and some are even offended by public displays of our animals. For this reason alone, I strongly discourage hunters from carrying their game home tied to the top of their vehicles, in the back of their pickup trucks with the tailgates down, or on their trailers. Not only does it not look good, but it also doesn't do much for the meat, either. Bug guts, road grime, and exhaust fumes tend to adversely "flavor" the meat, can ruin it, and actually hurt the aging process. Coolers work better at preserving the meat and keeping it out of sight. Use a lot of ice to keep the meat cold and to keep it from spoiling.

In some states, Texas for one, it is required that the head of the deer accompany the rest of the animal to its final destination. Since it is perfectly legal and acceptable for us to quarter a deer carcass in the field, the head is frequently detached. In such cases, I also discourage hunters from

Respect For Our Game Animals, Alive and Dead   125

publicly displaying the heads. I assure you, not all people are impressed by such gruesome displays.

Plus, if you plan to have your trophy mounted, any prolonged exposure to the elements in our environment only detracts from the final results. Just ask your taxidermist. Even they can only do so much when it comes to making a trophy look good. If you plan to proudly display your trophy on the wall, you will want it to look as lifelike as possible, and we owe it to the animal, too.

I've included some helpful tips on handling your trophies in chapter 22, Taxidermy Tips and Good Eating.

Squirrel Tales to Game Trails And Shore Lunches

16 Always Learning Something

As you have probably figured out by now, I am fascinated by wildlife, nature, and the outdoors in general. I don't believe there has ever been a time when I was hunting or fishing that I didn't learn something new. I continue to be amazed when a wild animal does something I've never seen one do before, or when I observe nature at its best, or worst. And I can honestly say that I have never seen the same sunrise or sunset twice.

I have only briefly touched on this subject in some of the previous chapters, but feel that I need to further explain why I feel the way I do. We are all different, thank God, and as such, we see things differently. I may take for granted something you take very seriously, and vice versa.

When I am hunting, I have the patience of a saint. I can sit in the woods from before daylight to after dark, never see a game animal, and yet totally enjoy myself watching birds or even livestock. I daydream. I may even read, but I totally enjoy the day. I don't take it so seriously that I fail to see and appreciate everything around me. In fact, as I've gotten older, I find myself procrastinating more and more, and have on several occasions come home empty-handed because I waited too long. Oh well. I also find myself passing up game late in the afternoon because I don't like cleaning and processing it in the dark. I like to think I've earned the right to do that.

What I haven't yet figured out, though, is why the same doesn't apply to fishing. When I'm fishing and the fish are biting, I'm having a great time. When the fish are not biting, I'm bored. Why is that? It's probably a good thing as far as my family life goes. You know what I mean?

I refuse to believe that wild animals cannot reason, at least to some degree. This reasoning is directly influenced by many variables, such as fear, hunger, noise, smells, terrain, and weather. Over the years, I've seen too many cases where an animal was able to solve a problem with no human intervention or conditioning. In fact, it was because we were doing something that the animal was forced to identify the problem, analyze the situation, and formulate a solution. I'll give you a couple examples that I have observed, and after reading them, I'm sure you will come up with a few based upon your own observations.

Since survival in the wild depends in large part on an animal's ability to successfully locate and gain access to a food source, it only follows that food is, in many cases, the reason animals do some of the things they do. It's one of the reasons deer, elk, turkeys, etc., will look for ways over, under, through, or even around fences. We hunters long ago recognized this fact also, and search out natural food sources to hunt near, such as acorn producing trees, grain fields, or orchards. Where it is legal to do so, we may even hunt over baited areas where feed is provided to attract game animals to an area where feed does not occur naturally. In this case,

Always Learning Something

however, it results in conditioning the animals to find food in certain areas that involve human action. Various seasonal food plots provided by hunters are a good example.

In Texas, we are allowed to hunt nonmigratory game animals over baited fields or around feeding stations. We are also allowed to hunt from concealment, both natural and manmade, and from the ground or elevated stands. These "advantages" greatly increase a hunter's chances of success, but also provide increased opportunities to just observe animals. It was while I was hunting from blinds overlooking feeders that I first realized how resourceful wild animals really are.

I'm always amazed and entertained by the antics of fox squirrels. They are true opportunists. They are inquisitive while at the same time cautious and boisterous at times, quiet at times, playful at times, vicious at others, and always greedy when it comes to food. I have often observed a squirrel expend a great deal of energy trying to prevent other squirrels from getting any corn at a feeder where there was more than enough to go around.

I usually provide a limited amount of whole corn for all the animals in the area I regularly hunt. I do this to ensure wildlife activity, be it game or nongame animals. This corn is dispensed from hanging basket feeders I made from hardware cloth and a wooden base. There is nothing automatic about them. The only way they drop corn is if I hit them with my hand as I walk past, or if birds and squirrels knock corn out of them. I suspend these feeders by rope from tree limbs so that they are readily accessible to me, yet out of reach of any cattle, horses, sheep, goats, etc.

Bear in mind now that these are wild animals, and as such, have never been exposed to birdseed or bird feeders in your backyard. They have discovered a new source of food in their backyard and have been able to take advantage of it. Now, of course, all the animals have ready access to whatever corn falls on the ground, but what if there isn't any on the ground? The deer just look up at the feeder and eventually walk away. The birds fly up and land on the wire mesh and help themselves to corn while at the same time knocking a few kernels to the ground. The squirrels are different.

I have watched squirrels go up the tree, out on the limb, and either jump to the feeder or climb down the rope to it. Once on the feeder, I have seen squirrels knock a few pieces loose, climb back down the tree, and then eat the corn they knocked down. I've seen others hang upside down on the outside of the basket and gorge themselves on corn. I also watched a squirrel go down inside the feeder, lie on his belly, and just pig out on corn. I then put a screen top on the feeders. He was not pleased and told me so.

The incident that convinced me that squirrels could solve problems, however, actually involved an automatic feeder that a fellow hunter had put up near his deer blind. The area was home to a large population of squirrels, so naturally they all wanted their share and as much of their buddies' shares as they could get. They were very greedy and would fight among themselves over more corn than they could all eat in a week. You were guaranteed to see squirrels if you hunted from his deer blind, and it was always entertaining.

Because the squirrels were so numerous, this hunter was spending a lot of money on corn that he intended for the deer and turkeys to eat. It was not uncommon for the squirrels to empty his thirty-gallon, hanging automatic feeder in two weeks, so he vowed to find a way to keep the squirrels out of the feeder. It soon became obvious that he may have met his match in wits.

He started by putting a shield on the cable he used to hang the feeder from a tree limb. It stopped the squirrels from

Always Learning Something

climbing down the cable, but they could still jump from the tree branches to the feeder. Once on the feeder, they would rake the corn off the feeder slinger and help themselves. Since the corn was gravity fed to the slinger, as long as they raked it, it ran out. I observed one rake the corn to the ground while the others fought over it on the ground.

The hunter then put a wire varmint guard around the automatic mechanism to prevent the squirrels from reaching the slinger. The guard still allowed the slinger to scatter corn whenever the motor was automatically operated, and it also allowed the hunter access to the "test button" on the motor. The purpose of the test button was to check the batteries and the unit for proper operation.

You guessed it. I suspect that the squirrel discovered the test button purely by accident while trying to reach the corn through the wire guard. I also suspect it scared the heck out of him when it started the motor running and corn went flying. I can only imagine that he was already running when he hit the ground, and that he didn't have anything nice to say once he stopped running. In any case, he had learned how to get corn out of the feeder, and all he had to do was push the test button. His ability to reason this out, and recognize that it wouldn't hurt him, led him to try it again, and again, and again.

The hunter, in the meantime, couldn't believe that the squirrels were still emptying out his feeder until he observed this squirrel reach through the wire guard and press the test button to dispense corn. Seeing that, the hunter shot the squirrel and as many of his buddies as he could. When I asked him why he shot them (I actually thought it was amazing and funny that the squirrels were able to figure out his feeder), he told me that he didn't want any of them teaching their friends bad habits. I think he realized he had met his match. It must have worked, because he never complained about squirrels eating all his corn again.

In a similar situation, I once observed five Jake turkeys feeding under one of my hanging basket feeders. There obviously wasn't much corn on the ground as four of the turkeys hunted and scratched in the dirt below the feeder. The fifth turkey stood back a few feet and intently stared up at the corn in the feeder hanging above them. I thought, "He's thinking about how he can get the corn out of the feeder." He was. Suddenly, he jumped into the air, flew up to the feeder, and kicked and beat the feeder with his feet and wings, knocking corn out of it. He then dropped back to the ground and quickly joined his friends in eating a few pieces of corn. He repeated this action several times over the course of the next half hour or so until I shot him. I didn't want him teaching his friends any bad habits, either. Tell me again that wild turkeys are stupid. He was tasty.

In both of these examples, I can't help but believe that these particular animals actually "reasoned" solutions to their problems, and I believe that wild animals in general are smarter than most people give them credit for. How else could they survive in the wild? Most survive where humans couldn't without a lot of help, and at the same time, many thrive in our midst. The whitetail deer and the coyote are prime examples. And besides that, if these wild animals weren't so smart, how else could we explain how they manage to make us look so foolish at times.

And then there's Mother Nature. No hunting or fishing experience would be complete without a lesson or two from her. Respect her, for she is very unforgiving to all who are careless, including us. If you venture out improperly prepared, or if you make a mistake or do something stupid, she can make your life very miserable if you are lucky, and take it away from you if you are not. She will also provide for you if you know where to look. She can be your friend or your enemy. Respect her and appreciate her for all she is.

As I get older and mature, I find I enjoy the simple things

Always Learning Something

more. It may be that I've slowed down, or because I take time to look around me. In either case, I like it. I've always liked the four seasons, but now they seem to be more vibrant, more intense, more fleeting. Cool fall days mean more than just another hunting or holiday season. They mean another year has passed.

I've started looking for a place to retire where I can be a little closer to Mother Nature. I want to see the sun rise and set on horizons clear of rooftops, power lines, and city lights. I like to think there are places left where a guy can do this. I hope there will be such a place for our children and their children's children. Take care of Mother Nature, and she'll take care of you.

Learning doesn't stop with observing wild animals, birds, and fish. I can't tell you all the things I learned while helping those two guys fly their floatplane off the Alaskan tundra. Some of those lessons I'd just as soon not remember. But if we pay attention to friends, fellow hunters and fishermen, guides, landowners, the weather, and, of course, the animals around us, we can learn a lot about a lot of things.

I've learned that most hunters don't really know how far away an animal is without a range finder. They also don't really know where the animal was standing at the instant of the shot, unless the animal drops in its tracks. I know this to be true because I've seen it happen too many times. The lesson here is to pay attention to those kinds of details before you pull the trigger or let the arrow fly. I have spent more than a few days over the years helping look for wounded animals. Two of them were my own.

In one case, a good friend came to where I was hunting and asked me to help him find a buck he had shot. I had him take me to the exact spot when he shot. While going there, he told me how he saw the deer, shot at it, and that it ran off and he couldn't find any evidence that he had even hit it. I had him direct me, from his spot, as I walked out to where he said the deer was standing. When I reached the spot, he told me to stop. That was the spot.

I asked him to stay where he was while I did a quick check of the immediate area for any blood sign. He had already spent a lot of time doing the same thing before he came and got me. As such, the area was so disturbed and messed up that I doubted we would find any evidence there at all. My first thought was that the deer really wasn't even there to start with. I started walking straight away from him in the direction he told me he shot. A full twenty yards beyond where he said the deer was standing, I found bits of deer fur and a lot of stomach contents. The deer was further away than he thought it was, and it was gut shot. We never did find that buck. My friend was a good hunter, and was devastated that we were unable to find his wounded buck.

Don't hesitate to ask for help finding a wounded animal. Expand your search area, carefully identify any sign you find to help you, and then formulate a plan to proceed.

In a similar situation, I was elk hunting in the Colorado Rockies a number of years ago with two friends of mine from the outfitter. It was a late season hunt and there was knee-deep snow everywhere, and more in a lot of places. We decided to drop down off a ridge into some thick cover in hopes of spotting some elk bedded up there. One guy would stay on top while two of us would very slowly slab off the top and down into the cover. The guy on top would spot for us and would whistle if he saw any elk from up high. We hadn't gone far when he whistled. We immediately stopped and couldn't see anything, so we proceeded very slowly. He whistled again, and this time he was a little more excited and pointing in a lot of different directions.

Then we saw what he was looking at. We had managed to walk right in among 'em, so to speak. We had cow and calf

Always Learning Something

elk all around us, so we didn't dare move. When he whistled the third time, he signaled that there was a 5x5 bull elk with them. About that time, all hell broke loose as the elk blew out of the cover and headed for somewhere else. I watched as a steady stream of elk went through a small clearing from my right to left, probably less than fifty yards away. I didn't see any bull with the ones already running out of the cover.

Then my friend whistled again and indicated that the bull was bringing up the rear and would cross the clearing soon. I got ready, and was aiming at the right side of the clearing when more elk broke across it. And then the bull ran out, and I tried to find his shoulder in my scope and fire at the same time. Then it was quiet. As we stood there, all three of us watched as elk continued to run up and over the top of the ridge behind us. None of us saw a bull go over the top. We all headed for the clearing to look for any sign that I had hit the bull.

There wasn't a square inch of snow in the clearing that didn't have at least one elk track in it. There also wasn't any blood. We decided that two of us would continue to look for blood sign while the other would follow the trail of tracks up the ridge and over the top to see what he might find. Hopefully, blood. He didn't go far, maybe a hundred yards, and whistled. He had found my bull, dead in the snow. The two of us walked over to where he was, had a round of congratulations, and admired my bull. We also discovered what had happened.

Since the bull was running, and the clearing was quite small, I was not able to actually "lead" the bull when I shot. My shot at his shoulder actually hit him further back and passed through his liver. He bled to death internally. That explained why we didn't find any blood sign.

As far as finding him goes, the two guides I was with knew that elk can carry a lot of lead a long way, and that he had only been shot once, if at all. They also knew that elk that were hit hard wouldn't go uphill because it hurts them to do so. They will typically go downhill, across any hillside, or even lie down. Since we didn't see the bull go over the ridge, my friend was sure that it was hit hard and we would eventually find it. He was right.

What my friend did was follow the route all the other elk had taken up the ridge. He never saw any blood. But when the elk started up the steep hillside, he found a single set of tracks that broke off the trail to the right and was headed across and down the hill side. He followed those tracks to where my bull lay dead. He never found a drop of blood along the way. When we opened the bull up to clean it, it was full of blood.

We gutted him out while one of the guides went to get the truck. Since you can't drag elk up hill, we dragged my bull down the hill to a two-track trail where our friend met us with the truck. It was dark when we got back to camp. By the time the story of my hunt had been told, we were all thrilled that these guides knew what to do and what to expect. Needless to say, we all learned a lot on that hunt.

Do you remember your mother or father, or possibly your schoolteachers, telling you to "pay attention, you might learn something"? It's still true today. Make it a goal to try to learn something new every day. The value and importance of learning is very useful in many ways and at many times in our everyday lives, as well as when we are hunting and fishing. Lessons learned are most valuable when you share them with others. Pass on your knowledge and experience to family and friends so that they can benefit, too. It could be as simple as telling someone about it, as in this book, or actually demonstrating it in an actual hunting or fishing situation.

Probably the best way to pass on your knowledge,

Always Learning Something

experiences, and lessons learned is to take them with you. A friend may be looking for someone to go hunting with. A spouse, son, or daughter may want to learn how to hunt or fish. Here's your chance to shine, to spend quality time with your friends and loved ones, and to possibly plant a seed of interest in them that could lead to enjoying many outdoor experiences with you.

Start off slow. Start with the basics and build up from there. Just let them share time with you at first. Don't rush it. As their interest evolves, you can add to their lessons and adapt their learning accordingly. Maybe they would rather fish than hunt. That's okay. Teach them to fish. Don't force them to hunt just because you want them to. Hunting isn't for everyone. You will turn them off if you persist in trying to get them into hunting.

Back before children (BC), my wife asked to go hunting with me one weekend. Of course I said great. We stayed in an old house we used as camp on a lease. She wasn't impressed. We got up early so we could be in the woods an hour before daylight. She wasn't impressed. I had to wake her up; she was in a sleeping bag to keep warm, to tell her we had a deer out in front of us. She wasn't impressed. And when I shot a deer the second day and field dressed it, and later skinned, quartered, and stripped the carcass for the cooler, she wasn't impressed then, either.

On the way home she thanked me for taking her with me, and was glad I enjoyed hunting so much. She also told me she had better things to do at 4:00 a.m. on any day of the week, but especially Saturday and Sunday mornings. It was called sleep. It was obvious she wasn't impressed, but she did tell me to have fun hunting. I always do.

Many years later, after our children (AC) were in high school and able to drive and fend for themselves for a week, I invited her to join me on a Colorado elk hunt so she could experience the beauty of the Rocky Mountains and meet my many close friends there. She did, and she did much better this time. Of course, all my friends catered to her every desire while we were there. And since the big ranch house we used for camp included all the necessary accommodations, she was more comfortable than during her hunt with me twenty years earlier.

We were up at 3:00 a.m., had a hot breakfast, and left camp at 4:00 a.m. We then hiked in the dark to where we wanted to be when the sun came up. She didn't complain, but I don't think she was all that impressed. By 7:00 a.m., we were watching elk move up into the hills around us to bed down for the day. At 7:30 a.m., I shot a 6x5 bull on the side of the hill across from us. She was excited for me until I told her the hunt was over and now the work begins, starting with getting over to the bull. We had to drop down to the bottom between us and then climb up the other side to where the bull was.

Due to the amount of cover and trees on both hillsides, our guide friend had us stay where we were while he went to the bull first. This was so we could direct him to the bull. He would then direct us as we made our way to where he and the bull were. This whole exercise took a couple of hours, but proved to be the most efficient process for getting to the bull in a timely manner. Did you spot the lesson here? You just learned something.

After the pictures and congratulations were taken care of, our guide friend called in to the others, both out hunting and back in camp, to let them know we had a bull down, where we were, and to request all the help they could provide in getting my bull out to the truck. We then gutted the bull and dragged it downhill to the bottom. Do you remember me telling you earlier that you don't drag elk uphill? Gravity helps you drag them downhill. They just don't cooperate if you try to drag them uphill. Another lesson learned? Even

Always Learning Something

so, they don't drag easily, even downhill, and I couldn't help but think how the snow had actually made an earlier bull drag much easier downhill.

By the time we got the bull to the bottom, help had arrived up on top. Two of our friends had brought a four-wheel drive ATV and chain saws to help clear a path up the hill and to the truck. It was now midday and the real work was just getting started. By the time the five of us and the ATV managed to get the bull to the truck and back to camp, it was dark and we were all hungry. There was a hot meal waiting for us, and all in camp were impressed with my bull and all the work it took to retrieve it. I know my wife was impressed, and she said so. She also thanked the guys, the cook, and me, and told us she was going to bed. She also made it perfectly clear that she would not be up early in the morning and to not wait on breakfast for her. She told us good night and to "have fun hunting tomorrow."

I got up early as always and accompanied my friends on their hunts, primarily as a spotter and workhorse. When we got back to camp that evening, dinner was ready and waiting. We were hungry. My wife was well rested and had enjoyed a leisurely day in camp. The owner, outfitter, head guide, and father of several of our friends there suggested that my wife and I go the next day to a lake on the property and catch some rainbow trout for dinner that night. He provided all the fishing gear and even a truck to get there. So we did.

It was a beautiful day and I knew exactly where he was talking about. When we got there and got our lines in the water, we started catching rainbows. By mid afternoon we had enough fish to feed everyone. My wife even insisted on cleaning her own fish, and I have pictures to prove it.

When we got back to camp and the cook took over, there was a little grumbling from a couple of our friends, the outfitter's sons. It seems that he usually didn't allow anyone, including them, to catch and keep any of the rainbow trout in that lake. He quickly explained that my wife was a lot better looking than they were, and that it appeared she was also a better angler than them. Of course this was all in fun and we sat down to the best meal of surf and turf ever. How can you go wrong with elk steaks and never even refrigerated rainbow trout with all the fixin's? There were no leftovers, everyone slept well, and we were all still talking about that meal the next morning. It doesn't get any better than that. Great friends, great food, and beautiful scenery. Sign me up every time.

During our feast that night, our outfitter friend suggested my wife and I take one of his trucks the next day and drive to Steamboat Springs, seventy miles away, so she could do some shopping and sightseeing, and have lunch while we were there. So we did.

We had a great day in Steamboat Springs, and made a return trip loop that afternoon through Meeker, where we were able to visit with a friend of mine who lives there. Then it was back to camp and another hot home-cooked dinner with our friends there. Life is good when you share it with friends.

We spent the next day getting our belongings together and ready for our return trip home. This included my bull's antlers. The meat was at a processer in Craig and would be shipped to our home when it was ready. The cost of the processing and shipment was on us, not the outfitter. It was well worth it when you consider the great time we had with good friends in some of God's most beautiful country.

The next day we were up early to say goodbye to everyone before they left to go hunting, and to thank them for their hospitality and hard work. A couple of hours later, after a leisurely breakfast, one of our friends loaded our stuff into his truck and drove us to the Yampa Valley Regional Airport

Always Learning Something

near Hayden, Colorado for our flight home. This was only appropriate since he was our friend who was with us the morning I shot my bull.

The meat is long gone, but the great memories will remain until I die. Make friends and memories. You can't go wrong with either. Then share those memories often. Life is short. Share it with friends.

In closing this chapter on learning things, I need to share something I heard a while back that answers a question we have all been asked at one time or another. This will especially make sense to those who know what an armadillo is. Those of us from Texas, and so many other southern states, are blessed with an abundance of these throwbacks to caveman hunters. They show up in the strangest places. Woods, yards, gardens, and towns. Everywhere it seems, especially along our highways, and usually smashed on them. So, here goes...

Q. Why did the chicken cross the road?

A. To prove to the armadillo that it could be done.

See that? You learned something from this book.

Squirrel Tales to Game Trails And Shore Lunches

17   Hunting Styles and Tactics

There really is no right or wrong way to hunt legally. Some ways work better than others certainly, but there is no right or wrong way to hunt legally. If someone tries to tell you there is, tell him or her that they are wrong. I'm living proof of it. In this chapter, I will share with you my ideas on the subject, as well as some others that I have observed over the years. Feel free to compare notes, so to speak, and if you see something that sounds interesting or makes sense to you, try it. Just consider it a return on your investment in this book. Another lesson learned?

Being an engineer, I tend to be very logical and attentive to details, as well as very practical and conservative. My wife can attest to that. I tell you this so you will understand what I am about to tell you. Did you get that? It makes perfect sense to me. Anyway…

My idea of hunting is to get outdoors, have a quality experience, hopefully see some game, and maybe even shoot something, in that order. In other words, I consider myself a true sportsman, someone who is somewhere between the "slob" hunter on the low end of the scale and the "fanatic" hunter on the other end. Please note that I didn't refer to the fanatic as the high end of the scale on purpose. In my opinion, the person who is obsessed with hunting, or fanatical about it, is missing out on the finer points of hunting and has carried the sport to the opposite extreme. If we applied my description to a bell curve, the slob hunter would be in the lower ten percent of all hunters, while the fanatic would be in the upper ten percent. The rest of us would find ourselves somewhere in the eighty percent in between. If you see yourself in that group, I consider myself in good company.

I am what I would describe as a casual hunter. I like to hunt, and I don't take the actual act lightly. However, I am not so serious about it that I will go to any length to be successful at it. Like I've said several times already, know your own limitations.

I've read almost everything I could get my hands on relative to hunting, and I came to the conclusion a long time ago that most of it is based upon individual opinions unfounded in fact that may or may not work under any conditions, let alone all conditions. Therein lies my second conviction: hunt the conditions. We have little or no control over Mother Nature or the elements. Therefore, if we choose to hunt, we must hunt under the conditions that exist at the time. If it's hot or cold, snowing or raining, windy or still, be properly prepared to hunt the applicable conditions. The same applies to fishing. Don't whine about the conditions or how they affect your hunting. Adapt to the conditions you have.

My hunting is, for the most part, limited to weekends, and there are only so many of those during any given hunting season. In order to maximize those opportunities, I have invested in a good ground blind that I hunt from when

Hunting Styles and Tactics

hunting deer and turkeys on leased property. It permits me to be as comfortable as possible under all but the worst conditions, and even allows me the luxury and space for a companion to join me. My daughter, Kyle Marie, and my son, B. J. have hunted with me in this blind on several occasions, and Kyle Marie shot her first whitetail buck from it. Not only does this blind provide for a more comfortable hunt, it offers excellent concealment as well. I find it much easier to stay on stand all day if I am at least comfortable.

You have probably heard it said that the three most important elements needed for a business to succeed are location, location, and location. I'm here to tell you that the same elements are needed when you hunt whatever, wherever, and how. Think about that. If you want to hunt deer or elk, you need to go to where the deer or elk are to be successful. I could sit in the best blind ever made; wear the best camouflage clothing available; shoot the best rifle money can buy; use scent block, doe-in-heat and buck-in-rut scent lures, and decoys; put out all sorts of fruits, vegetables, grains, and attractants; and sit there all day, every day, for the rest of my life and never see a deer or elk if I did it in my back yard where I currently live. Do you see my point?

Your chances of being successful at hunting are greatly increased if you at least hunt where whatever it is you're hunting are known to live. You can further refine the location, and increase your success, by concentrating your efforts around areas game is known to frequent within where they live. And to further enhance your chances, position yourself in a location that offers concealment and the minimum chance of being smelled or heard. These are all good reasons to consider a guided once-in-a-lifetime elk or big game hunt. Just remember location, location, location. Reputable guides can make your hunts a memorable experience and increase your chances of success.

As an engineer, I have found all of this, so far, to be quite logical. Due to the limited size of our deer lease property, I have placed my blind in an area where deer are known to be. The blind provides comfort and limited concealment under most conditions. This combination has proven to be quite successful for me over the years. Too bad it doesn't help me with my fishing.

On the other hand, from a strictly practical standpoint, I don't see much need in my case to wear a lot of camouflage clothing since I'm concealed in a blind. I also don't see much need in using a lot of scent covers on deer that are used to smelling, seeing, and hearing man on a regular basis. The deer on our lease see, smell, and hear our landowner every day when he makes his rounds to check the livestock he has on his property. They are so used to seeing him, they don't even run when he drives through the pastures. When I'm hunting I try to be quiet, I usually wear camouflaged, or at least a dark-colored shirt or coat, I scatter a little corn around the area, and I may or may not use a small amount of cover scent. That depends on how warm it is that day. Other than that I have not seen any positive results from rattling, grunting, or using the various scent attractants so I don't use them. That's not to say that they don't work at certain times of the year or in some areas. I'm just saying that I have seen little or no benefit from their use.

We had a fanatic that hunted with us for a few years on our lease in the Texas Hill Country. He had also read everything ever written about deer hunting, but he believed every bit of it, too. He carried everything to the extreme, and would not listen to reason or admit that there were other ways to hunt. It was actually kind of funny in a way, and it drove him nuts that I hunted so casually, yet consistently did better than he did. The key to it all was that I had selected an excellent location and he was not able to identify one, try as he may. He firmly believed that if he put out enough feed, the animals would come to him, so he insisted on putting

Hunting Styles and Tactics

his blinds in areas that were easily accessible to him with no regard for natural deer needs. He never did figure it out.

In comparison, as an example, I put my blind in a natural funnel area where deer moved through, while he put his next to the two-track road because he had seen a deer cross there once. At the time, my blind was a well-used wooden box with holes cut in it with an ax for windows and a door. He had built a wooden box blind, painted it inside and out, had flaps over the windows, and only used peepholes to peek out of when checking for deer. I had two hanging basket feeders in my area, while he had two automatic electric feeders. I wore a camouflage shirt, blue jeans, and a cowboy hat while he hunted in full camouflage, including face paint. I kept my clothes in the camp house, while he hung his outside in a plastic bag with a sprig of fresh cedar in it. I took a thermos of coffee and a lunch into my blind. So did he. But when I needed to relieve myself, I got out of my blind, did it, and got right back in my blind. He relieved himself in a bottle in the darkness of his blind, and then emptied the bottle when he got back to camp later. In three consecutive years, I took both my bucks on opening morning within an hour or less of each other from my blind, a feat he never did once. He hated it, especially since I had to drive past his blind on my way back to camp. I loved it.

In thinking back on it, this guy was worse than a fanatic. He was a self-proclaimed expert on everything. All you had to do was ask him. He would tell you. He knew it all. Remember those automatic electric feeders I mentioned earlier? Well, he built those himself, but not without a great deal of time and effort. The basic idea was good, but after many engineering hours and attempts that only failed for one reason or another, he recruited another fellow hunter to help him with the electronics. Their combined efforts also proved to be inadequate, so they broke down and bought a commercial feeder, which they duplicated by buying the various electronic components and manufacturing the rest. This is commonly referred to as reverse engineering. I still believe that even after all that, they spent more time and money building their own feeders than if they had just bought them to start with. Oh well, you couldn't tell either of them anything anyway, and they would never admit they were wrong. It was their time and money.

This guy was fanatical about everything. He had the opinion that his rifle was the perfect rifle for everything, and that his hand loads performed better than anyone else's, including factory ammunition. If you shot any rifle other than what he shot, you were not as likely to do as well as him, and he let you know it. He was successful in influencing several other hunters to change their rifles or loads, even though they had very adequate equipment for hunting Texas whitetail deer. Oh, by the way, this guy had a Federal Firearms License, and could buy and sell guns. Think about that for a minute.

We had a "gadget man" that hunted with us, also. You've probably seen or known people like him. He had a gadget for everything, and every time something new came out, he was the first to have it. I once watched him clean a deer and he had no less than five knives, each with a specific use, and he used each one in the process. After he was done, I kind of felt inadequate, but only for a minute or so, and then the feeling passed. He was the first among us to purchase a handheld GPS (Global Positioning System) so that he would always know where he was. He was another one of those guys who had more money than sense. Oh well, it was his money. Back then those GPS units were very expensive.

And then there was the Wild Man. This guy also wore full camouflage, including face paint, underwear, and even toilet paper. I wondered if he used face paint to camouflage his butt so the deer wouldn't see it. We'll never know, and it's probably better that we don't. He was something else. He had taken deer with a rifle, pistol, black powder, bow

Hunting Styles and Tactics

and arrow, and shotgun. He had even found a deer caught in a barbed wire fence and put it out of its misery with a knife. Nothing strange or wild about that so far, huh? Well, when he said he wanted to jump out of his tree stand on to the back of a deer and kill it with his bare hands, or at a minimum a knife, I said I wanted a part of that action. That's right. I wanted to sell tickets because I figured that would be really exciting, at least for a little while. What do you figure a ticket to that action would be worth? Other than this small obsession, the wild man was kind of normal.

I had the pleasure of hunting a few times with an older gentleman who was retired and who dearly loved to hunt. He had worked with guns all his life, and had actually hand made several black powder rifles that he hunted with. He had arthritis so bad that he couldn't sit for any length of time, so he hunted by slowly moving through the woods. I watched him once and I swear it took him over an hour to go a hundred yards. But he always got his deer. In fact, one time he shot two deer with one shot through the necks. He knew his limitations, and I never knew him to miss or wound an animal. Oh yeah, he was a heck of a good fisherman, too.

He also chewed tobacco all the time, even in his sleep. He kept a can by his bed so he could spit during the night. I don't know how he did it. He would take a shot of Wild Turkey Bourbon before going to bed to help him sleep, and another shot in the morning to get him started. It was probably the only way he could wash the tobacco taste out of his mouth.

Over the years, I've had the chance to hunt with a few women. Besides my daughter, one other woman was a real joy to hunt with. Both she and her husband hunted with us one year, her first ever deer hunt. She was so excited to be there, it was like I was on my first hunt, also. As it turned out, when she shot her first deer, her husband wasn't there. She brought her deer, a doe, to the house, guts and all. I don't know how she got it in the back of their Jeep, but she did. She was so excited that she couldn't stand it. I helped her clean her first deer and told her I hoped she had taken good notes. I only do one, even for her.

She only hunted with us the one season. If I remember correctly, she shot another deer or two, and I believe hers were bigger than her husband's. The next year she was pregnant and couldn't hunt with us. I gave her husband a real hard time about what he had done in order to prevent her from showing him up again. He swore it wasn't planned that way, but I still don't believe him. She's always welcome to hunt in my camp again.

When it gets down to hunting styles and tactics, there really is no right or wrong way as long as it is legal, within reason, and conforms to fair chase. Check the Boone and Crocket Big Game record book for their complete definition of fair chase, and keep it in mind when you go hunting for your trophy of a lifetime. If you succeed, but fail to comply with their definition, your trophy will not be recognized or included in "the Book." It could be a new world record, but if you poached it or shot it behind a high fence enclosure, too bad. It may have cost you a fortune. Too bad. This falls under chapter 15, Respect for Our Game Animals, Alive and Dead.

Even if you are not trophy hunting, styles and tactics vary greatly. One example includes a bunch of good old boys getting together to drink and play cards half the night and then go out the next day at noon to see if they can find something to shoot. They are away from their jobs and their wives for a week and intend to make the most of it. If they do shoot a deer, they really only want a meal or two of venison. They give the rest of it away, or it goes to waste.

Another example is the guy who can't really take any time off to hunt, so he goes out early opening day and "gets it

Hunting Styles and Tactics

over with." He shoots the first deer he sees and is glad that is done with so he can get back to business.

Both of these examples are perfectly legal. They both also miss the point and are lacking in many basic elements of real hunting. These would not be good examples to teach your children.

There's also the example of the hunter that won't kill any animal unless it meets his high expectations. It has to have so many points, be at least so wide or tall, be so many inches, or be over so many hundreds of pounds. These guys are very selective, and that's okay. After all, it's their time and money.

Then there's the guy who only hunts a few days during the season, but he's bound and determined to "limit out," even if it means shooting yearling deer. He filled his tag, but not his freezer. Again, it's his time and money, and as long as it's legal, all are happy. It just seems to me to be a waste of time and money.

I hunted with a guy like this years ago. He was a very good guy, had two boys he was teaching to hunt, and would usually have them with him. When it got to the last weekend of the season, he would show up with a tag or two not filled. He would shoot whatever it took to fill his open tags. I referred to these deer as briefcase deer because you could pick them up with one hand and put them in the back of his truck. He was not teaching his sons a good habit. I even joked with him by telling him that he was one heck of a shot to be able to hit such a small deer. He just laughed. He didn't care. It was legal.

I touched on an example of tactics earlier in this chapter with the guy that was fanatical, and how I was pretty much the opposite but always seemed to be more successful. Again, so long as it's legal, so be it. He did kill a rattlesnake under one of his feeders once.

If elevated stands over automatic electric feeders in the middle of food plots in an enclosed, heated blind is your thing, go for it as long as it is legal where you are hunting. If ground blinds or tree stands are your thing, go for it. If these enhance your hunting experience, if not your success, it's worth it. Just make sure to know and comply with any rules and regulations that limit what you can and can't do.

Many years ago, I hunted in a state that only allowed hunting on the ground and natural concealment. You could not alter in any way, shape, or form any natural materials to improve your concealment. You could only use it "as is." Now that's spartan and challenging. But that was the rule.

If you prefer stand hunting, still hunting, or glassing and stalking; if you prefer public land or leased property hunting; if you enjoy day hunts or package hunts; and even if you choose to hunt high fence enclosure hunts, just know and obey the rules. The tactics are different for all of these and will define the level of difficulty in each, and will result in a certain level of satisfaction for you.

I did a high fence enclosure hunt a few years ago with several friends. It was my first and last such hunt. We were there to hunt "wild" hogs. The only thing wild about them was they were caught wild, penned up in a one thousand square yard enclosure, and they were not happy about it. Beyond that, we were taken into the enclosure, assigned a place to hunt from, and told not to leave that spot.

The operator then chased the "wild" hogs around the enclosure and past each hunter, who could then pick one out and shoot it. There was absolutely no sport or hunting involved. It was nothing more than shoot and kill a hog. No tactics were involved whatsoever. It was not my idea of hunting or fun.

In that same enclosure were two 5x5 bull elk that just stood quietly side by side in the middle and watched all

Hunting Styles and Tactics

the action. I asked the operator about them before we left. He told me they were already paid for and that the hunters would be there in a few days to shoot their trophies. In other words, to kill them and take the meat home and have the heads mounted. No fair chase in that high fence enclosure. No hunting, either, just killing.

As I mentioned in an earlier chapter, my daughter has hunted with me a few times at her request. A few years ago, she asked to go hunting with me, so we did. She has always been a good shot, but had never shot anything except targets. On our first hunt together, I shot a buck and she helped me clean and process it. The next year, we didn't shoot anything while she was with me. The next season, she shot her first buck, and now says I have a hunting partner for life. I can handle that.

As you can see from the above, it takes all kinds, and that's just a few of the people I have hunted with over the years. I'm happy to say that I would gladly hunt with at least eighty percent of those people again.

Squirrel Tales to Game Trails And Shore Lunches

18 Fishing

Finally, huh?

It's probably a really good thing that I'm not an avid fisherman, too. I mean, think about it. I don't have enough time or money to hunt as much as I'd like to now, so I don't know when I'd find time to fish, too. Plus, to me, fishing is boring unless the fish are biting. And besides that, it wouldn't make sense to own a boat I didn't have time to use, and I don't have room in my garage to store one for indefinite periods of time anyway.

There may come a time when I want a boat to go fishing, but I really doubt it. If I do, I'll rent one. I figure I'll save a lot of money that way. I know too many people who said the second most wonderful day of their life was the day they bought their boat. The first most wonderful day was the day they sold it. They all describe their boats as a hole in the water they throw money into, or as a great place to store things in their garage. One guy told me he had even forgotten he owned a boat until one weekend when he cleaned out his garage and found it in there. Now that's bad. What was worse, though, was all the stuff he found in the boat that he had long since replaced because he couldn't find it when he needed it. If you ever saw his garage, you would believe him, too.

I felt it necessary to devote at least one chapter in this book to sharing my fishing experiences with you, limited as they may be. I realize that many hunters are also fishermen in the off-season, and that some even manage to find time to go. Don't get me wrong. I go every chance I get. It's just that I don't get a lot of chances. Maybe if I owned my own boat? No, that isn't going to happen. I just did the math and do you know how many fish you have to catch and release to pay for a boat? It's mind-boggling.

I have been fortunate enough to fish for salmon in the Great Lakes, Alaska, and the Pacific Ocean. I have been deep-sea fishing in the Atlantic Ocean, and I have caught brook trout in streams in Michigan and Vermont. I've caught bass, walleyes, perch, lake trout, sunfish, bluegills, northern pike, Arctic char, rainbow trout, Arctic grayling, smelt, muskie, halibut, red suckers and probably a few more types of fish over the years from Alaska to Texas and from

Fishing

the east coast to the west coast. I do like to fish. But like I said, it's probably a good thing that I don't have more time to fish than I do. It would tend to cut into my already limited hunting time, not to mention my family time.

I remember as a kid growing up in Michigan catching brook trout in a tiny stream that ran in a ditch along a gravel road. Those fish always tasted so good, and were a real treat when we caught them. They never got much over twelve inches long, but I still believe that, pound for pound, they have to be the best fighting fish I have ever caught. A number of years ago I had the opportunity to join my best friend in Vermont for a few days of fishing, and we spent most of our time catching "Brookies" in creeks that ran in ditches along gravel roads. It was a wonderful time, it brought back a lot of great memories, and it reminded me how good a breakfast of fresh brook trout, eggs, and toast tasted. Like the commercial says, "It doesn't get any better than that." My best friend recently passed away, and although we never did get back up to Vermont to fish for Brookies again, every time we were together we talked about that trip and how we really needed to do that again. Too bad we didn't make it happen. I miss him.

After catching and keeping brook trout, it was hard to catch and release king salmon that weighed forty pounds or more, but I did. We were only allowed to keep three fish, and the kings were running up river to spawn. We were in Alaska and out in what had to be, in my opinion, the most beautiful place on earth. Bald eagles and bears were taking advantage of the salmon buffet at the same time we were, but the limits didn't apply to them. No one in our group was even willing to try to explain it to them, let alone try to enforce it.

I have mentioned meals of fresh fish and want to make clear that what I mean is fish that has never been frozen. In some cases, these fish were so fresh they never saw the inside of a cooler. These are meals that can be at home, in camp, or on the shore of the lake or river. The best fish I have ever eaten were during shore lunches where the fish were caught, taken to shore, cleaned, cooked, and consumed all in one sitting. There is just something about a fresh salmon or trout wrapped in tin foil with a little onion, seasoning, and butter, and cooked over an open fire outdoors in the fresh air that can't be beat.

As a kid, we would spear red suckers in creeks in the spring, and we'd fix them the same way, because the fish would cook off the bones. Throw in a few small new potatoes and you would swear you had died and gone to heaven. Even those red suckers tasted good fixed like that, especially after a night of spear fishing and cleaning suckers. Mom would can the rest of the suckers and we would eat them throughout the year. We called them the poor man's salmon patties. All I know is that they tasted really good to a bunch of hungry kids, and we were thankful to have them.

It's a real rush to catch a nice rainbow trout on a fly rod on a river in Alaska, but to me, it was an even greater rush to spend an afternoon with a bunch of kids helping them catch rainbow trout in a stream-fed pond in Colorado. I was thrilled that they all caught fish and had a good time doing it. Those kids are all grown up now, but still remind me how much fun they had when I took them fishing. It was a lot of fun. Try it some time.

To start with, fishing comes in many forms and methods, and can be found in one form or another anywhere in the world. And much like hunting, it also includes many styles and tactics. And in the case of wanting to fish for a specific type of fish, just like in hunting, you will need to go where that species is available. The biggest difference with fishing is that you need to decide if you want to fish for freshwater fish or saltwater fish. That narrows down your choices, locations, and type of tackle, and drives all related costs. Be

Fishing

prepared. Just like hunting, there are many choices and the sky is the limit. Or should I say the water is the limit?

If you've never fished before, or you are only an occasional fisherman or woman, and especially if you own little or no tackle and have no clue as to where to go fishing, consider just chartering a fishing boat for a few hours or even a whole day. All you usually need to bring with you is your checkbook, a sweater, suntan lotion, sunglasses, and possibly a cooler of cold drinks and sandwiches.

Every person that plans to fish will need a fishing license, and the captain of the boat will direct you to where you can purchase that. Everything else is normally provided with the charter boat, and usually includes cleaning any fish you catch and want to keep. If you tend to get seasick, you may want to take that into consideration. Everyone else with you on the fishing trip will greatly appreciate it.

Just like hiring an outfitter and guide for a more enjoyable hunt, hiring a fishing boat will not only save you money in the long run, but the captain will also know where to find the fish, have the right equipment to do so, and will make every effort for you to have an enjoyable and successful day of fishing. After all, this is their livelihood and they want you to come back again. Make sure you choose reputable charter boats, ask questions, and ask for references if you are uneasy with the operation.

I love to fish in Alaska. They have so much to offer and the scenery is unbelievable. This is not to say that everywhere else I've fished isn't beautiful, but I have fished to the sound of traffic, airplanes, and screaming children and adults. I've fished creeks and rivers where cattle stood and watched us the entire time. I've fished streams where you fought your way through brush just to get close to the water. And then there are insects, but they seem to follow me wherever I fish.

Fishing

There are so many kinds of fish and locations to fish in Alaska that you may find your only competition for salmon are the bears fishing with you. That can happen. I have a picture I took of a bear fishing just across the river from where I was fishing. My fishing pole is in the picture. He seemed to be catching more fish than I was, but I was not about to use his style or technique. The water was way too cold for me.

On another trip, we were catching and releasing chum salmon. The natives refer to them as dog salmon because they feed them to their dogs all winter long. I asked if there was a reason the locals didn't eat them and was told that king salmon, silver salmon, and sockeye salmon were all much better eating due to chum salmon being much oilier (And we pay good money for omega 3 found in fish oil supplements). He did say that dog salmon was very good smoked because of all the oil in it.

We were only allowed to keep three salmon on that trip, but I did keep one nice chum salmon and when I got home, I smoked it and it was delicious. If I remember correctly, my other two salmon were silvers, sometimes called Coho salmon. They were delicious, too, but I'm glad I kept the chum salmon and would do it again in a heartbeat. Don't be afraid to try new types of fish. Another lesson learned?

I mentioned earlier how I dearly enjoy a shore lunch of fresh-caught fish that have never seen the inside of a cooler, let alone a refrigerator or freezer. I usually have aluminum foil, a small onion, a stick of butter, and salt and pepper in my backpack, especially on fishing trips in the wild.

I was on one such fishing trip several years ago in Alaska and we were specifically fishing for king salmon. There were probably a dozen people in camp, including a party of four or five Japanese businessmen. When we all arrived back in camp, we took our fish to the cleaning tables and were all

Fishing   161

busy cleaning and filleting our own catches. I happened to be standing next to one of these gentlemen at the cleaning table. Although I couldn't understand a word these guys were saying, I couldn't help but hear the excitement in their voices as they talked and laughed while they took care of their catches. When I looked over to see what they were so excited about, I noticed that they were all carefully shaving thin pieces of fresh king salmon, splashing it with soy sauce, and eating the freshest sashimi you could get. Several of them had brought soy sauce with them just for this purpose. The gentleman next to me offered me his soy sauce. I graciously thanked him and joined them in a feast of the freshest sashimi I have ever eaten. My fishing buddies thought I was crazy, and in not so many words, told me so. They really missed out. Too bad.

Lesson learned. I now include a bottle of soy sauce in my backpack pantry just in case I get a chance to enjoy a good meal of fresh salmon sashimi with my shore lunch. And in case I chance to meet that Japanese gentleman again, I'll be able to return the favor. I still don't know what he said, but he said a mouth full as far as I'm concerned. Be prepared and have high expectations.

On a related note, as I talked about always learning something in chapter 16, this is specifically related to a fishing excursion to of all places Dillingham, Alaska. It starts with you really have to want to go to Dillingham in order to get there. It's one of those small communities in Alaska that is landlocked, and cannot be reached by roads. You either get there by boat or you fly in. I was there to go fishing for a week. I do not know what other commerce there is in Dillingham, but there are obviously limited opportunities at the airport and on the shipping docks. There is probably at least one grocery store, maybe a hotel or two, possibly a church or two, and even a school. And then there are the fishing lodges that cater to people like me. All I can say is the fishing was great, the accommodations were very nice, and the people were super.

I talk to everyone and I'm always asking pertinent questions if I'm in an area I've never been to before. Since this was my first trip to Dillingham, I was talking to our van driver on the way from the airport to our lodge. He told me the drive was only about nine miles and that half of it was two-track roads. This fact caught my interest, especially since I already knew that Dillingham was landlocked. So when I asked him how many miles of road there were in Dillingham, I wasn't surprised that he knew. What surprised me was how he answered my question. He simply said, "There's thirty-two miles of improved road, sixty-four if you decide to come back." That certainly puts it in proper perspective, doesn't it?

Did you know that? Well now you do, and you can say you learned something today. You're welcome.

Somewhere in a box somewhere in our home are pictures that I took when our kids caught their first fish. I really need to locate those and put them in a scrapbook for each of our children. I always do a better job of keeping pictures of my hunting and fishing trips together than I do of their pictures. One of these days I'll do it, only it will take more than one day to do. Talk about bringing back memories, huh? I've done a much better job of keeping up with pictures of our grandson.

Squirrel Tales to Game Trails And Shore Lunches

19   Comfort

As I get older, comfort and convenience have more of an influence on my decisions of where, when, and how I hunt and fish. The idea of sleeping on the cold ground in an unheated tent in the snow just doesn't have the same appeal as a heated cabin or lodge with warm, comfortable beds. But then, as I "mature," my primary reason for hunting and fishing has evolved from "getting my limit" to a relaxing, enjoyable, and quality experience. I've realized that a freezer full of meat isn't as important as the memories, and doesn't last as long, either.

Each camp over the years had its own intrinsic features and level of comfort, as well as lasting memories. Some were certainly more comfortable than others. I'll always remember each for the times I enjoyed there, from the community house in Michigan to the old farmhouse in Texas, from the cook tent in Oregon to the condo in Vermont, from the lodge in Alaska to the ranch house in Colorado, from the tent on the tundra to the back of my pickup truck, and everything in between. Each served a purpose beyond its intended use. Each housed and nurtured camaraderie between people with mutual interests: between friends, and between fathers and sons and daughters.

Comfort should extend beyond the campsite. With all the modern equipment available today, a person can stay warm and dry for extended periods of time, even when exposed to the elements. Where blinds are permitted, even greater levels of comfort are possible. That deer blind in Texas, or the ice-fishing shanty in Michigan, is now liable to include all the comforts of home, limited only by one's imagination and checkbook. And why not? Where does it say you have to be miserable when you're hunting or fishing?

We now have rifles that shoot farther, faster, and flatter than ever before. We have bows without cams, with one cam, with two cams, and with pins for this and that. We have shotguns and pistols with scopes. The pistols, in some cases, are nothing more than fancy short rifles, and even shoot the same cartridges. And the scopes now gather more light, tell you the range, and even have lighted crosshairs.

Comfort

The only things they don't do yet is calculate wind speed, wind direction, and elevation, and then automatically make the corrections needed to hit a running deer at a thousand yards. I guarantee it is coming, though. It's just a matter of time. The point I'm trying to make is that we have so much to choose from that there is something out there for everyone, even the southpaws and those with physical disabilities. Isn't it wonderful?

As much as I enjoy shooting my open-sighted rifles, my deteriorating eyesight requires me to use a rifle with a scope on it when I hunt. I'm told it's a result of age and that I need to get used to it. So, unless I'm hunting in heavy cover, I usually use a rifle with a scope on it. I guess I'm just a little old-fashioned, or remember the good old days. There's nothing wrong with that. That's where the memories were made.

I always carry a camera with me on my hunting and fishing trips and have taken a lot of pictures over the years. I have pictures of most of the places I camped and the lodges where I stayed. I have pictures of my trophies, animals, birds, flowers, sunrises, and sunsets. I have pictures of my hunting and fishing friends and associates. Several of them have since passed away. I miss them.

One of my favorite pictures is of a trapper's cabin somewhere in Alaska. I was up there fishing and just happened to notice a smokestack sticking up out of the grass along the river as we drifted past. I had to stop just to see what was up there. It was worth the stop and effort.

I say up there because we were fishing a river that rose and fell with the ocean tidal changes. This particular river rose and fell at least twelve feet each time the tide came in or went out. We happened to be at low tide at the time, so I had to climb up the steep riverbank in order to reach level ground along the river. The grass was about three feet tall and partially obscured the cabin.

When I got close enough to see it, I realized it was a trapper's cabin. The more I looked at it, the more I was amazed. Even though cabins can't talk, this one spoke volumes and told a very clear story about it and its owner. Although it was very simple and minimal, it was extremely functional. The more I studied it, the more I noticed, and the more impressed I was with it and its owner.

When I got my film developed after I got home, I had one picture enlarged and framed. It's on the wall in my basement and never fails to generate interest from people when they see it. Their first question is always, "Where is that at?" I tell them it's in Alaska and ask them to look closely at it. It's only after they don't notice anything special about it that I tell them the story, tell them what they are looking at, and point out several key features that put it all in perspective. Then they are amazed at what they are looking at.

It looks like a cabin, complete with a door and a chimney. But when I point out that this log cabin is only about three logs high and only about four feet tall at the peak of the roof, they realize this is a very small cabin. I estimated it was only about six feet wide by eight feet long. Most people's bathrooms are larger than this trapper's cabin. Then I point out a blue, five-gallon PVC bucket lying next to the door in the forefront of the picture. All of a sudden they have perspective. They now realize just how small this cabin is. The door is just large enough to get in and out. There are no windows, and there is no lock on the door. I point out the recent addition of a new, unweathered piece of plywood fashioned as a windbreak next to the door to minimize snow drifting in front of the door. He even has a much weathered moose skull and antlers on the roof above the door.

Inside is a dirt floor with a raised mound of dirt just to the left inside the door and in the corner. It is a fire pit with

Comfort

a piece of steel over it and a chimney to vent the smoke. It's the smokestack I saw from the river. When he builds a fire in the pit, he can warm water for coffee or even have a hot meal. There is just enough bare ground to spread out a sleeping bag. The fire also helps take the chill off in the cabin. And that is all there is to it. Very simple yet very functional, a shelter in a storm left unlocked for anyone else to use should they need to. Talk about comfort, huh?

And you thought you knew what roughing it was like. He used the blue bucket to get water out of the river or to collect snow. I only saw the one bucket.

The roof was pieces of corrugated steel, like you see on barn roofs, so it would allow run off of rain or snow. It was probably a cold cabin, even with a fire in the hearth, but it was pretty dry and out of the elements. It was probably the most comfortable place anywhere around there when the weather was bad.

In his later years, my dad got to where he liked to go fishing once in awhile. He never did fish very often, but he did seem to enjoy it when he did go. I don't think he ever really cared if he caught anything or not. I once asked him to go hunting with me sometime, and he laughed and said that it was always too cold for him when the hunting seasons came in the fall and winter. He went on to say that when hunting season fell in June, he would be happy to go with me. Once again, it was a case of comfort, his. I miss him. We never did hunt together.

Squirrel Tales to Game Trails And Shore Lunches

20 Safety, Rules, Common Sense, and Limitations

I don't know about you, but my first deer hunt was fifty years ago. I've also done a lot of hunting and fishing since then. I still do a lot of planning and preparation prior to actually heading off to the hunt. Years ago, we didn't have cell phones. Nowadays, we don't leave home without them. How did we survive without them? Years ago, I wasn't on any medications, now I can't leave home without them. Years ago, I was invincible. Not so much anymore.

Simply because of the nature of the activities, hunting and fishing require a real attention to safety. Think about it. We tend to go to remote areas, some in very rugged terrain where a slip or fall could hurt you or even result in death. There can be critters out there that can bite or sting you or worse yet, kill you. If you hunt out of an elevated stand, you expose yourself to the risk of falling out of it. You can get lost or caught up in extreme weather conditions, either in camp or away from camp. When hunting in remote areas, even if you were able to call for help, you could die before help reached you. Cell phones are a lot of help, but even they have limitations. Many areas don't have good service if they have service at all.

A GPS is nice, but it has batteries in it that can go dead. Depending where you are when it happens, or you lose it, you could die. Do you know how to use a compass? A small survival kit in your backpack could mean the difference between life and death if you find yourself stranded in extremely remote areas.

We take for granted a lot of the equipment we use. Most have operating instructions, including basic rules of safety. All guns do, yet we get so used to handling them that we get sloppy or complacent and forget to unload them, or point them at someone by mistake. When this happens, the risk of an accident increases dramatically. An accident of this nature, out in the middle of nowhere, can be fatal. Follow the safety rules on all your equipment, and refresh your memory every season before you use it the first time.

All of these points should be common sense and become second nature to us. But many of us only hunt a few days a year, and shoot even less. Some don't take their boat out on a regular basis, and when they do, they realize they forgot something or do something stupid. Refresh your memory on the rules, regulations, and safe operation of your equipment before you use it each time. Rules and regulations are known to change regularly, and ignorance is not an acceptable excuse.

Know your own, and your equipment's, limitations.

If you haven't practiced three hundred-yard shots on

Safety, Rules, Common Sense, and Limitations

targets, don't try three hundred-yard shots on live animals.

If you can't hit a target at forty yards with your bow and arrow, don't take any shots at live animals at or beyond forty yards.

If you are a poor judge of distance, get a range finder and use it before you shoot with a rifle or bow.

If you have a physical limitation that prevents you from performing all the physical requirements of your hunt, don't do the hunt. It's for your own good. No one wants to have to drag your remains out of the woods to the truck. I admit that I can't hike the Rockies the way I did thirty years ago, let alone ten years ago. My health limits my capabilities. Does yours? Be honest with yourself.

Outfitters and guides will want to know your limitations before you hunt or fish with them. Own up to your own limitations before you do a big do-it-yourself hunt. If you do have a problem, there won't be anyone there to drag your remains back to the truck. Think about it, and be honest with yourself. It might help you have a more enjoyable and even successful trip. You will increase the chances of your survival, and you and your loved ones will be happy about that.

Always tell someone where you will be and when they can expect you back. This is good advice for all hunters and fishermen, whether hunting with a group of friends or a guided outfitter, and especially if you are hunting alone. If your plans change during the hunt or fishing trip, notify those persons and update your plan with them. It's for your own good. It will help them know where to start looking for you if you don't return when you said you would. That alone might be the difference between life and death.

Years ago I managed a thousand acre deer lease in the Texas Hill Country. In Texas, one thousand acres is very small. When you find yourself turned around and it's getting

172 Safety, Rules, Common Sense, and Limitations

dark out, most people will panic. Suddenly, a thousand acres can seem like a thousand square miles. Believe me, it's true.

When I took over the management of this deer lease, the first thing I did was draft a list of rules, including dos and don'ts for the benefit of every hunter on the lease. The second thing I did was get a topographical map of the area that included this property. I enlarged it to where only the deer lease property and its boundaries were clearly identified on a huge piece of paper. I then added the location of every known deer stand on the property, and clearly marked all roads, creek crossings, gates, and structures. I also made name pins for every member of the lease. The map went up on the wall in the kitchen, along with all the name pins.

One of the rules was if you were on the lease for any reason, your name must be on the map where you intended to be, even if you were not hunting. This served several purposes. Someone arriving at the camp could look at the map and tell if anyone else was there, and where they were hunting. That way, when they went out to hunt, they wouldn't disturb others by blundering through the area they were hunting in. It also told them who the others were that were there, and where to start looking when someone didn't get back to camp as expected. This is a good idea if you are hunting on leased property with others, if you are hunting unfamiliar property, and especially if you are hunting alone anywhere, anytime.

In the fourteen years that I was involved with this lease, we went looking for missing hunters on several occasions. In a couple of cases, the person was turned around in the dark. In a couple of other cases, we helped a fellow hunter recover the deer that they had shot right at dark and couldn't find. In every case, the hunter was relieved when we found them and helped them out. In every case, we at least knew where he was supposed to be and where to start looking for him. I love happy endings.

Squirrel Tales to Game Trails And Shore Lunches

21 Slobs, Clowns, and Products

I briefly mentioned slob hunters in chapter 17, Hunting Styles and Tactics, on purpose. Since I believe they only comprise about ten percent of all hunters and fishermen, I chose to concentrate on the other ninety percent of us in that chapter. I also chose to address them here because it's a broader problem than just slob hunters. In fact, I'm concerned that some TV hunting shows promote what is clearly not actual hunting or safe hunting practices, and sponsors promoting such programs and hunters are giving the rest of us a bad reputation, and even provide ammunition for the antihunting groups. We don't need to help them with their cause.

Having briefly described my hunting style and some of my tactics, I'll admit that I have no time or respect for slob hunters. These are the guys that make the rest of us look bad when they hunt. On the other hand, though, I find fanatic hunters almost entertaining with the extremes they go to. But I mostly enjoy the company of the other eighty percent of hunters who are serious, conscientious, safe, and courteous.

We have all known slobs. They may have been a fellow employee, a neighbor, a family member, or a best friend. Since I'm specifically addressing hunting, I'll not go into any areas other than hunting, except to say that I find all slobs to have one thing in common. They seem to have a blatant disregard for rules and regulations. This has nothing to do with being neat, clean, or even organized, and can certainly apply to anyone, no matter how educated they are.

I have hunted with several slob hunters over the years and have had to tell them they were no longer welcome on our deer lease. In one case, the guy insisted on not following the rules he agreed to. In another, safety was compromised and I refused to ignore a potential accident. In these cases, the parties involved thought they were "pulling a fast one" on the rest of us. We enforced the rules and did not let them back on the lease. Both of these hunters were educated, respected, and professional businessmen that should have known better. Both had broken more than one rule more than once.

In trying to fill openings on our deer lease, we usually selected someone one of us knew based upon a personal recommendation. We also conducted a very informal interview in an effort to ensure that we were getting people who would accept our rules for what they were. This process worked most of the time, but not always. Occasionally, we would get a hunter, or hunters, who talked a good story, but couldn't back it up with actions.

We had two guys that hunted with us one season who claimed to be "great white hunters" with lots of experience with deer, elk, etc., and pretty good shots. When they finally got a chance to demonstrate their skills, it quickly became obvious that I had not asked the right questions during their

Slobs, Clowns, and Products

interviews. As it turned out, all they had ever done was actually shoot the animals. Someone else had cleaned and processed them. They had only hunted on package hunts where the guide or outfitter did all the work except pull the trigger. Please don't get me wrong, though, I'm not bad-mouthing packaged hunts. The guides and outfitters get paid to gut your animal. These guys did not even watch it be done, let alone help. They didn't have a clue.

It was kind of funny because this came to our attention the first day of the season they hunted with us. It was already dark out, and several of us were already back at camp and fixing dinner for everyone when these two guys came in from hunting. When they pulled up with a deer in the back of their truck, none of us gave it a second thought. I was kind of surprised though that they had not at least cleaned the deer in the woods. But then again, it may have been too dark to see after they shot it. It wasn't the first time a hunter brought a whole deer back to camp to clean and put it up. Remember the lady I mentioned in a previous chapter? It happens.

But I became a little more suspicious when these two guys hung their deer upside down in the tree before they cleaned it, and then got out a book and began to read how to clean, skin, and quarter a deer. After they got it half opened up, they decided to let it down and rehang it by the neck while they finished cleaning it. They then had a real mess on their hands, feet, clothes, and everywhere else within ten feet of them. It was not a pretty sight, and it was getting late. Bear in mind, this was all happening in the light of a single floodlight. I thought maybe when they decided to rehang the deer by its neck, they had been holding the book upside down and had finally realized their mistake.

Another hunter and I had been watching this whole comedy unfold in total disbelief. It was at this point that we decided one of us had to help these two clean and process their deer before they ruined it, and before they hurt each other. An hour later, their deer was cleaned, skinned, quartered, and on ice, and the mess was cleaned up. I told them that I hoped they had paid attention and had taken good notes because we only do that once. I also told them where they could take the gut pile to dispose of it. That was pretty funny, too. I don't remember if they shot anymore deer that season, but they didn't come back the next year. I guess they couldn't stand the sight of blood and guts. Both of these guys were highly compensated professionals that had more money than sense, and I suspect they went somewhere else to hunt where all they had to do was shoot the deer. We didn't miss them.

You probably know a slob hunter or have hunted with one at some time. They are among us, and they are not only rifle hunters or bow hunters or muzzleloader hunters. In most cases, they are one in the same and hunt by all methods. Most tend to prefer one method over the others, but a slob with one, is a slob with all of them.

Some slobs don't even shoot their rifle, bow, or muzzleloader before hunting with it. Then, when they miss a shot, or only wound an animal, they tell you it was hitting dead-on the last time they shot it last season. This comment alone confirms that the person didn't check the gun, at a minimum, and didn't practice with it, either. Hopefully, he missed the animal completely.

The same is even more important for slob bow hunters. These are the guys who put a bale of straw in their backyard a day or so before they go hunting and believe that as long as they hit the bale, "that's good enough." The kill zone on a deer is not the size of a bale of straw. And how long a shot was it? If it was twenty yards away, where do they think it'll hit a deer at thirty or even forty yards? Will he take shots longer than twenty yards, or even fifty yards?

Slobs, Clowns, and Products

Like the rifle hunter above, just being "on the paper" at a hundred yards, or hitting a bale of straw at twenty yards, is not good enough. Proficiency with a weapon does not mean taking a shot or two at a paper plate the day before you go hunting. The same applies to muzzleloader hunters and handgun hunters.

All these typical weapons have specific limitations, and if you choose to hunt with any or all of them, know their limitations, and more importantly, know your own limitations with each of them. If you are not proficient with it, don't hunt with it just because you can.

I do not hunt with a bow and arrow. I made a conscious decision on this matter many years ago and have not looked back. I believe we have progressed beyond poking holes in animals with a pointed stick for obvious reasons. Guns are more efficient, more accurate, and typically more humane in the hands of proficient hunters. Even with the advancements in modern archery equipment, the limitations, not the least of which is the archer, still do not impress me. They are still, for all practical purposes, a primitive weapon, even considering all the so-called improvements that only tend to blur the definition of a primitive weapon. And even with all the latest improvements, the fastest arrows and most bizarre arrowheads, it still comes down to the person hunting with it. The limitations of the bow itself must be well known and never exceeded, no matter how big the trophy is. The increased "challenge" of archery hunting should never compromise that decision. The arrow is still only going to travel at approximately 350 feet per second, and only has a realistic effective range of approximately forty yards. Add to that the fact that it is slowing down and dropping fast, accuracy is, at best, less than ideal.

The term "primitive weapon" is also applied to black powder and muzzle-loading rifles. Talk about blurred lines, especially with muzzleloaders. You can now buy muzzleloaders that break over and allow breach loading of the powder charge. It is a muzzleloader only in that the projectile is still loaded from the end of the barrel. As far as the projectile goes, most are now rifled sabots, and even solid copper bullets in a plastic sleeve to retain it in the barrel and to center it down the barrel when the gun is fired. All of these features are intended to improve accuracy and range. Why not just hunt with a rifle in the first place? Round lead balls are pretty much limited to the true black powder rifles.

Modern muzzleloaders come with almost as many options as you have when buying a car. Smooth bore or rifled bore? Stainless or blued barrel? Black or camouflage synthetic stock? Primer cap or electronic ignition? End plug or break over? Open sights or scope? And more. Some are advertised to be accurate out to two hundred yards and beyond. How far is beyond? How much energy is left in the projectile at two hundred yards and beyond? Most slobs don't think about that and also don't hesitate to take a shot.

Muzzleloaders have evolved so far from what some people and states consider a primitive weapon that they clearly define the primitive weapons they will allow and won't allow to be used to hunt animals in their states. Check the rules and regulations of the state you plan to hunt in before you leave for the hunt. You may be surprised. Your modern muzzleloader with all the whistles and bells may be legal in your home state, but may not be allowed in another.

In case you haven't figured it out yet, I also don't hunt with black powder or muzzleloaders. I prefer the option of at least one follow-up shot, if needed, and especially if I am hunting where some of the animals hunt back. I shot my last bull elk at three hundred yards with a modern rifle. I would not have seriously considered a shot had I been using a modern muzzleloader. As it was, my one shot kill was so well placed that the bull went five yards and collapsed. I didn't even need a second shot, but I was prepared in case

Slobs, Clowns, and Products

I did. Remember what the guide told us before our first elk hunt? Elk can carry a lot of lead a long way. If the elk doesn't go down, shoot it again, and keep shooting until it does go down. I had already chambered another round in the time it took my bull to go five yards. Do that with a muzzleloader.

All I have to say to you handgun hunters is, why? I really can't come up with any good reason to hunt with a handgun. I know there are people who do, but I can't understand why. When I see an average hunter hunting with a typical over-the-counter handgun, in any caliber, I wonder if they know anything about ballistics. I also wonder if they are proficient with it and know at what maximum range to shoot.

Don't get me wrong, though, there are some professionals that hunt with a special type of handgun. It is usually a heavily modified rifle with a pistol grip. It is single shot, shoots a rifle bullet, and has a much longer barrel than most pistols. They are closer to a sawed-off rifle then they are to a pistol. Most are bolt action and even sport a high dollar scope. Is that really handgun hunting?

When you buy a handgun to hunt with, you need to know that you have a severely limited weapon. Severely limited as in almost useless, as in slow and very limited in effective range. We're talking in feet, not yards.

Due to the short barrels on handguns when compared to rifles of the same caliber, muzzle velocities aren't even close. And neither is accuracy or energy downrange beyond about twenty yards. Depending upon the specific load, some handguns have a muzzle velocity of less than one thousand feet per second. That is slow. I have a pellet rifle that pushes a .177 pellet at one thousand feet per second at the muzzle. True, some handgun loads have higher muzzle velocities up to 1,200 to 1,350 feet per second. But you need to remember that very few animals are shot at point blank range, and that all bullets start slowing down and losing energy, as well as accuracy, the instant they exit the barrel. Handguns just happen to be especially bad about it.

Have you ever wondered why when police and bad guys get into shoot-outs, a lot of shots are fired and only a few ever hit their target? I have. And I know that even though the police routinely qualify with their service weapon on stationary targets at known distances under calm conditions, it isn't that way at all in a firefight that's much over twenty feet with the bad guy on the move and shooting back.

I don't hunt with a handgun, either, because I know its limitations. When I'm hunting, I don't want a handicap.

I touched just briefly on why I don't hunt with a bow and arrow, muzzleloaders, and hand guns, and they all have something in common. They are all relatively short-range weapons. As a result, to be effective and successful when you hunt with them, you need to get as close to your target as possible before you decide it is within the range of the weapon and your ability to hit your target at that range.

The latest fad or craze among so-called hunters is the long-range shots. This appears to be driven by the success of military snipers on enemy targets a mile or more away. Of course they have spotters and state-of-the-art rifles and scopes, some of which are not available to anyone outside the military. They are also trained on the equipment and how to shoot under extreme conditions. There is a good reason why the military has snipers. And they practice a lot.

The guys that are in to this long-range hunting have the best equipment currently available, and have even practiced making long shots. They are also setting a poor example for every slob hunter and hunters that should know better. There are just too many variables that affect long-range shots that they don't know, understand, or even care about. Things like trajectory, crosswind components, thermals, bullet drop, humidity, caliber, bullet muzzle velocity, and

Slobs, Clowns, and Products

velocity on target to name a few.

These slobs are happy shooting out-of-the-box rifles and using the cheapest ammunition they can buy. And just because someone on television is making thousand-yard shots, he thinks he can, too. And that's where it gets ugly and starts to look more like killing than hunting. Remember, this is the slob that won't spend much time looking for an animal he shot at a hundred yards. He sure isn't going to spend much time looking for an animal he shot at four hundred or more yards away. He'll just assume he missed it and continue hunting. Maybe he did miss. What if he didn't? Just because some rifles and optics are capable of very long shots doesn't mean the guy doing the shooting is. If you insist on shooting long, keep it on the rifle range and don't use living animals as targets.

I also have a problem with most of the hunting shows and some of the fishing shows on television. I think a lot of them are sending the wrong message about hunting and fishing. Unfortunately, the slob hunters that watch these shows get part of the message loud and clear and completely miss the real story.

Although these "actor" hunters don't advertise the facts, the truth is that most of them arrange hunts every week with outfitters that don't charge them to hunt on their property in exchange for endorsing their hunting property. The host hunter of the show also never has to do any prehunt preparation. He, his camera crew, and hunting buddies show up at the camp house the day before they hunt, sight in their weapons, eat, and go to bed.

The outfitter manages the property for hunting purposes. He has food plots in key areas, permanent stands along known travel routes, and lots of game cameras with pictures of every animal in the area and the time of day or night they show up at the feeder.

The next day starts with the host hunter leaving camp for a specific hunting stand where his cameraman is all set up and the two of them wait for the animals to show up. All the viewer ever sees is the actual shot and the celebration after it. If they actually find the animal, they spend a lot of time "buttering each other's bread" (a Texas term) about how good the hunt, trophy, and outfitter was.

That's not hunting. That's killing. And because of their sponsors, they made a lot of money doing it. And then they head off to the next prearranged hunt location to repeat the process and film the next week's show. And so on, and so on, and so on. No one, especially the slob hunter watching the show, learned anything about hunting. All we saw was the star of the show shooting an animal. You can't help but wonder what we didn't see. What was cut out and not shown? What happened to the meat? We can only hope it was properly processed and went to good use. The host hunter is only in it for the money and the antlers, and nothing else.

Please don't get me wrong, though, I didn't say all hunting shows are like this. There is a few that do a much better job of filming actual hunts and all the effort and work that goes into them. But there are only a few. Most have evolved to where the host hunter or hunters, the so-called stars of the show, spend more time clowning around and acting like fools than they do hunting. That alone sends a very bad message to antihunter groups that all hunters are slobs, clowns, or fools, and only care about killing animals. There is no place in hunting for such antics, especially on television. Keep the horsing around off camera and concentrate on the how-to, the hunt, and specific points that will help the observer become a better hunter. Oh, that's right. I forgot that these hosts don't do any of those themselves. They just show up, shoot an animal, and then move on to the next "hunt."

That brings me to sponsors and their choice of product names. They don't seem to help our cause by coming up

Slobs, Clowns, and Products

with some very grisly and descriptive names for their products. Is it possible they compete to see who can come up with the worst name for a product? But then they really aren't as interested in our cause as they are in selling their product, or else they wouldn't come up with these names or even sponsor some of these clowns out there. It all boils down to nothing more than names and advertising that sells their product to hunters. It's purely a business decision.

Here are a few examples of actual product names. You will probably recognize most of them. I'm sure all are registered trademarks and copyrighted.

Bone Collector, Raptor, Cremator, Lok'd & Lethal, Blaze, Sniper Lite, Fang, Enforcer, Wicked Ridge Invader, Vindicator, Lazer Strike, Killzone, Wac'Em, Torrid, Deer Season, and Extractor.

Really? What's wrong with this picture?

It's also not necessary. If they build a good product and it meets all the demands expected of it, it will almost sell itself. Performance speaks loudly. Vindicator? Really? Most of the animals we hunt are totally defenseless against us.

There is one product I want to mention, because it really worries me, and it speaks to some of my concerns about where we are headed with our sport. You may have already seen it advertised, but when I saw it, I couldn't help but think we've gone too far with this one. It's an arrow that incorporates a bullet in the tip to fire upon contact and discharge a projectile into the animal to increase damage to it. Why not just use a rifle in the first place? Am I missing something here? So much for a primitive weapon. I can't believe it. Where will it end?

Hunting should test your wits and skills against an animal in its own free range, natural environment and surroundings. Any unfair advantage on our part to that effect makes it nothing more than killing. Ethics do matter.

In wrapping up this chapter, I want to tell you about a televised hunt that I saw recently. This was an elk hunt that demonstrated many of the very points I just discussed. To start with, the hunter was waiting for the elk to stand up so he could take a four hundred-yard shot at it. Four hundred yards is a long shot by any standard. Could he have gotten a little closer? Of course he could have, and should have. When the bull elk did finally stand up, the hunter took his shot. The shot hit the bull, but it was high and way back. The shot broke the bull's back. As the bull tried desperately to stand up, the hunter took three more shots at it. Three. Apparently, the fourth shot hit the bull and he went down. Then the congratulations and glad-handing started.

What especially made me mad was when the guide told the hunter what a great shot he had made. All of this was on camera and televised. It was not a great shot. It was a sloppy and lucky shot at best. If the shot had not broken the elk's back, would they have had anything to celebrate? Would they have even televised the hunt?

Squirrel Tales to Game Trails And Shore Lunches

22 Taxidermy Tips and Good Eating

Through the course of my hunting and fishing career, I never had a trophy mounted by a taxidermist. I simply mounted the antlers on wooden plaques that I made myself. This included elk, caribou, mule deer, and whitetail deer. Some mounts were small while others were huge. They all looked nice.

I was also known to process my own deer, unless I didn't have time to. I would always keep the back straps and tenderloins, and take the rest to a processing plant and have it ground into burger. All of it. And I specified no suet, fat, or pork to be added. Just ground venison burger.

It's a good thing our kids liked venison, wild turkey, elk, and more, because we ate a lot of it over the years. They still eat it when they are here, and usually take frozen burger and my homemade venison summer sausage home with them. My homemade jerky is always a hit with them, too. I never got fancy about certain cuts or sausage or jerky because I always made my own. No bones went in the freezer, only burger and back strap. I made the summer sausage in twenty-pound batches from the burger. Nothing went to waste.

Then, about eight years ago, I decided to go to taxidermy school. It was a great four-week course. I then got my licenses and started mounting animals. As a taxidermist, you are trying to make every mount look so alive that you expect it to breath and move. It is truly an art in every sense of the word.

In doing taxidermy, I developed a series of tips to help hunters and fishermen who plan to have a trophy mounted know how to handle it, and what to do and not do. I've included them here for your information. I've also included a few tried and true recipes that work with either venison or elk. Enjoy. Please feel free to season them to your liking. We like them as written. Please consider these tips and recipes a return on your investment in this book.

Great Bird Mounts Start With You

Do's and Don'ts to Help Your Taxidermist Produce the Trophy You Expect

If you plan to have your trophy bird mounted:
- Don't handle your bird any more than is necessary after shooting it.
- Don't clean/gut your bird.
- Don't hold the bird by the neck.
- Do attempt to limit the amount of blood on the feathers.
- Do be careful not to bend or lose any plumage, such as head, neck, wing, and tail feathers.
- Do keep your bird refrigerated if you plan to have it mounted.
- Do get your bird to your taxidermist within three (3) days of shooting it.
- Do bag and freeze the whole bird if you do not plan to drop it off at your taxidermist within three (3) days of shooting it.

If you are not going to mount your bird, you do not need to follow any of the above steps.

Just remember, if you leave it in the freezer too long, the skin can get freezer burn and could ruin it.

Great Fish Mounts Start With You

Do's and Don'ts to Help Your Taxidermist
Produce the Trophy You Expect

If you plan to have your trophy fish mounted:
- Don't handle your catch any more than is necessary after catching it.
- Don't clean/gut your catch.
- Don't wrap your catch in paper or plastic.
- Don't freeze your catch.
- Do take pictures and record the measurements of your catch if you plan to release it and have a reproduction made. Record its length, width, and girth at three-inch intervals along its length. Also record its weight.
- Do keep your catch in a live well if possible.
- Do keep your catch in a cooler in cold water while in transit home or to your taxidermist.
- Do get your catch to your taxidermist within three (3) days of catching it.

If you are not going to mount your catch, you do not need to follow any of the above steps.

Just remember fish, and relatives, begin to stink after three (3) days.

Taxidermy Tips and Good Eating

Great Mounts Start With You

Do's and Don'ts to Help Your Taxidermist
Produce the Trophy You Expect

If you plan to have your trophy mounted:

- Don't shoot it in the head or neck.
- Don't cut past the bottom of the sternum when gutting it.
- Don't drag it out of the woods behind your ATV or truck.
- Don't hang it up by the neck.
- Don't hang it up to "age the meat" with the hide on it.
- Don't attempt to cape the animal unless you know what you are doing.
- Don't remove the antlers unless you know what you are doing.
- Do shoot the animal in or behind the shoulder.
- Do cut the hide around the animal at or below the sternum.
- If you cape your animal in the field, do cut the hide up the center of the back to within twelve inches of the antlers.
- Do carefully skin the neck and shoulders to remove the cape up to the base of the head. No holes if possible.
- Do cut the head off the neck without cutting the cape.
- Do carefully roll the cape up with the hair side out, and bag it to keep moisture in and dirt out.
- Do get it to your taxidermist ASAP. She/he will gladly

finish removing the cape and antlers from the head.

- Do take it to your taxidermist before you take it to be processed if you need help skinning and caping your animal.

If you are not going to mount your animal, you do not need to follow any of the above steps.

Just remember, if we treated good beef the way some hunters treat their wild game, it would taste gamey and be tougher than an old boot, too.

Chicken Fried Venison Steak Bits

This recipe is best if you use venison back straps, tenderloins, or steak muscles from the hindquarters.

Trim fat and sinew from the meat. Cut the meat lengthwise in long strips approximately two inches thick and two inches wide. Then cut these strips across the grain in pieces approximately a quarter inch thick.

Mix up a meat wash of several eggs and a splash of milk. Put meat pieces in mixture and stir until all the pieces are thoroughly wetted.

In a large zip-lock bag, mix two cups of white flour, a tablespoon of garlic salt or powder, a tablespoon or two of sugar, and a half cup portion of corn meal (optional). Quantities of these ingredients will vary based upon the amount of meat you are fixing. Add additional seasonings of choice if you wish.

Remove meat from the egg and milk wash and put them in the bag of flour mixture and shake it until the pieces are well coated.

Remove the battered pieces of meat from the bag and fry them in hot cooking oil until lightly browned. This can be done in a deep fryer or a frying pan. Do not overcook.

Carefully remove meat from the hot oil and put it in a large bowl that has been lined with paper towels to drain before serving. Repeat the process until all the meat has been cooked. Use a paper towel between subsequent layers of meat for good drainage.

Best if served hot. Can be microwaved if there are any leftovers.

Enjoy.

Venison Summer Sausage

(Single batch makes ten pounds)

7 lbs of pure ground venison burger (no fat added)

3 lbs of pork breakfast sausage (I use regular)

10 tsp Morton Tender Quick Salt

5 tsp course black pepper (regular pepper is okay)

2 tsp hickory smoke salt

5 tsp mustard seeds

5 tsp garlic salt or powder

½ cup white Karo syrup (optional)

Mix the venison burger and pork sausage together and then run it through a meat grinder to ensure texture consistency. If you don't own a meat grinder, mix it by hand and make sure it is mixed thoroughly.

Add the seasonings, hand mix it well, cover in a container, and refrigerate it.

Take it out once a day for three days and hand mix it well, always refrigerating it afterward.

On the fourth day, divide it into ten rolls, and roll them out until they are about ten inches long. Lay them on cookie cooling grills in cookie trays to catch any drips. Leave a space between each roll to allow for heat circulation when cooking. I spray the grills with Pam to make the cleanup easier. I also line the cookie trays with aluminum foil to catch any drips. I rarely get more than a few drips in any pan.

Bake for eight hours in a preheated oven at 175 degrees, turning the rolls every two hours during the process. I try to ensure they cook with a different side up each time I turn them to ensure thorough cooking. I also swap them between

Taxidermy Tips and Good Eating

oven racks during the process to eliminate effects of possible hot spots in the oven(s). Do not overcook.

After cooking, remove from the oven and let cool before wrapping the rolls in Saran wrap or putting them in baggies for the freezer or refrigerator. Since they are fully cooked, they can be frozen for later use.

I suggest you slice a roll fresh out of the oven. You will be amazed at how tasty it is.

Note: This recipe is very mild due to the seasonings I use. We love it. If you want to spice it up for adult tastes, go for it.

Enjoy.

Ben's Venison or Elk Jerky

2 lbs of steak, back strap, or tenderloin

¼ cup Teriyaki sauce

1 tbsp Adolph's Tenderizer Salt

1 tbsp Hickory Smoked Salt

1 tbsp Mixed Up Salt

1 can of light beer

Combine the ingredients, except for the meat, in a large bowl.

Trim the meat to remove fat and silver skin.

Slice the meat into strips about 1/8 inch thick.

Mix the meat into the marinade, cover, and refrigerate overnight.

Preheat oven to 170 degrees.

Put foil in drip pans and put cookie cooling racks in the drip pans. Spray them with Pam.

Lay the strips of meat on the cookie cooling racks in a single layer.

Put trays of meat on oven racks and leave the door slightly open to allow moisture to escape.

Allow the meat to dry in the oven for four hours, or until it bends without breaking or moisture in the bend. Thicker slices may need to dry a little longer.

Finished jerky may be refrigerated or frozen. Makes about one pound of jerky.

Enjoy.

Squirrel Tales to Game Trails And Shore Lunches

23   In Closing: Concerns

By now you know a lot about me, and how I feel about a lot of things relative to hunting and fishing. If you read between the lines, you know more about me than you think you do. And if you have stayed with me this far, we probably have a lot in common, and to some degree, share the same concerns for our sport and its future.

I have a problem with the fast-paced lives we live and the schedules we keep. We don't have time to hunt and fish anymore. We're too busy trying to make a living, raise a family, and get ahead so that we can someday, hopefully, relax and enjoy ourselves. The only reason I don't hunt squirrels still is that I'm so busy, there just isn't time. I have difficulty finding time to hunt deer and turkeys a few weekends each year. It's even harder to find a week to hunt elk. There's something wrong with that.

What's even worse, my wife and I are not spending the time we should with our own children and grandchildren.

In Closing: Concerns

We are not able to introduce them to the outdoors, our sport, and to let them experience with us some of those wonderful times. Instead, they only hear negative opinions expressed by people bent on eliminating our sport. It is a shame that they are not allowed to form their own opinion because they have not been exposed to both sides of the issue of hunting. Not only do our children and grandchildren miss out on the hunting experience, but game animals and ultimately all wildlife could suffer.

I know that hunting isn't for everyone. As an example, both of my children have hunted deer with me. My daughter has killed her own buck, while my son doesn't care to hunt again. They both like to shoot, and they shoot very well. If my son doesn't want to hunt, I'm not going to force him to. Since my daughter expressed an interest in hunting, I made it possible for her to do so. If she chooses to never hunt again, it's all right with me. I'm pleased that she was interested in hunting, and I never tried to discourage her from doing it just because she is a girl. I'm proud of both of my children.

Beyond the actual hunting experience itself, I'm concerned about what we are leaving our children and their children's children. We must do everything in our power to preserve and manage large, wild areas that are accessible to all for the enjoyment of nature. We must protect those areas, and ensure that they are available for many generations to come. Everyone should have the opportunity to hear a loon call at sunset, to hear a wolf howl in the wild, to watch the northern lights dance, and to enjoy a sunset over the horizon unobstructed by man-made objects.

Hunting and fishing are an important part of our heritage, and have been proven time and time again to be the most efficient, effective, and humane method of wildlife management. We must work together to prevent losing the right to hunt and fish, and ensure generations to come the

In Closing: Concerns

opportunity to experience hunting and fishing. We must all remember that there is much more to hunting than killing.

With that, I offer my sincerest hopes that all your hunting and fishing trips are as enjoyable and as successful as mine have been. Make great memories and share them often. Good luck, shoot straight, and remember to keep a tight line.

Squirrel Tales to Game Trails And Shore Lunches

24   One More Thing to Think About

Remember back in chapter 11, My First Caribou Hunt, where I described in great detail how two guys flew a small airplane out of the frozen lake on the tundra? Well, needless to say, I've remembered it many times over the years since it happened. And the more I think about it, the more I wonder about all that beer they consumed in the process. What part did it play in this event?

In looking back on it, I can't help but think the beer was an integral part of the overall plan all along. Don't laugh. Like I said, I've thought about this many times over the years and over a few beers.

Here's what I think. The beer may have actually helped them hatch the whole plan in the first place. The alcohol may have helped them "think outside the box" while discussing their limited options.

On the actual day of execution, no pun intended, they may have started drinking beer early in the day in order to prevent them from changing their minds. Canned courage, so to speak. As the plan progressed, they may have been drinking the beer in order to build up their courage to go through with the plan.

Believe me; I'm not trying to make up excuses for those guys or to condone their actions. The fact that they had come up with a crazy, yet viable plan, would indicate that the beers were not talking the loudest.

The fact that they were both pretty well "feeling no pain" at departure time again may have been a necessary part of their plan, too. Just in case. After all, what if they crashed on takeoff? The beer would ease any pain, and they would have died happy. Very happy, actually.

But what if they survived the crash on takeoff? The beer would have served as medicinal pain relief, kind of like morphine.

And if they didn't survive the crash on takeoff, the beer in their systems would have acted as antifreeze and embalming fluid, preserving their remains until they could be recovered, or until the bears ate them and copped a good buzz off the alcohol.

On a positive note, the beer they took with them may have been a toast to their successful plan and takeoff while cheating death and destruction one more time. All are worthy of a celebration.

I'd hate to think it was just because the beer was available and free.

Hopefully, they had a safe landing, and here's wishing all of you a safe landing in everything you do. Cheers.

www.ingramcontent.com/pod-product-compliance
Lightning Source LLC
Chambersburg PA
CBHW070138080526
44586CB00015B/1739